Praise for *No Greater Love*

In a time of such profound loneliness and isolation it's hard to think of a more urgent book than this one. The health of our churches and strength of our witness are both bound up with our understanding of the beauty and importance of the kind of friendship Jesus is inviting us into. This is the most significant book I've read in many years.

SAM ALLBERRY, associate pastor, Immanuel Nashville; author of *7 Myths about Singleness* and *Is God Anti-Gay?*

Friendship is a dying art. In an age in which any strong emotion toward another person is interpreted as romantic or sexual, Rebecca offers Christians a much-needed corrective. Not only can we love one another deeply and genuinely, we must. Where else will the world witness the priceless-ness of a friend who sticks closer than a brother, if not in the church? Imagine what a light in the darkness we would be if we committed to love one another and to love our neighbors as only those unbound from the fear of relational loss can do. *No Greater Love* gives us an excellent place to start the work of reclaiming the essential art of Christian friendship. I absolutely loved this book.

JEN WILKIN, author and Bible teacher

I haven't read a book on friendship in a decade, and this felt so fresh. Whether you are single or married, young or old, male or female, this is the book you need to read this year. Rebecca demonstrates that friend-ship is a lost art and the missing element in most churches. Its absence robs every other part of our lives. This is a delightful, important, and (crucially) biblical book.

J.D. GREEAR, pastor, The Summit Church; author of multiple books, including *Essential Christianity*

T0017700

We crave authentic friendships where we can be known, accepted, loved, and challenged to grow. Most of us have experienced the pain and heartache of friendships that have not delivered what we expected. In *No Greater Love*, Rebecca offers us a transparent, vulnerable, and challenging view of the costs and benefits of biblical friendships, and their necessity for our spiritual growth and witness in the world. This book will cause you to rethink popular notions of friendship and encourage you to pursue God's plan for healthy relationships.

CHRISTINE CAINE, founder, Propel Women & A21

Every so often a book comes along that masterfully weaves together the compassion of Christ and the spiritual muscle of practical theology. *No Greater Love* does this through Rebecca's real-deal wisdom regarding friendship. Readers will be discipled and helped in the beautiful calling to lay down our lives for each other as friends.

ELLEN MARY DYKAS, director of Equipping for Ministry to Women, Harvest USA; author, *Toxic Relationships: Taking Refuge in Christ*

I know of no one better to write a book on friendship than Rebecca, who is the very best of friends. Though she would be quick to protest and point to her failures, the people who love her and have been loved by her will testify that everything she writes here, she lives. But this is not a book about Rebecca; it is a book about what is available to us in Christ, our supreme, unfailing friend. No matter what your past experience has been, you will find encouragement, hope, and conviction in these pages to take the risk of deep friendship and enjoy its reward.

RACHEL GILSON, writer, speaker, and author

For far too long, many Christians have been taught that friendships are a luxury. Rebecca has written the most compelling case for why the church should see friendships as absolutely central to spiritual formation and the biblical vision of the Christian life. In the spirit of Bonhoeffer, *No Greater Love* challenges our minds and hearts to take seriously the gospel's call for us to embrace life together. This is a must-read for every Christian leader.

CHRIS BROOKS, Senior Pastor, Woodside Bible Church

a Biblical Vision
for Friendship

NO
GREATER
LOVE

Rebecca
McLaughlin

Moody Publishers
CHICAGO

Edited by Connor Sterchi
Interior design: Brandi Davis
Cover design by Erik M. Peterson
Cover illustration of hand copyright © 2023 by kkgas/Stocksy (4797115). All rights reserved.

ISBN: 978-0-8024-2892-9

Originally delivered by fleets of horse-drawn wagons, the affordable paperbacks from D. L. Moody's publishing house resourced the church and served everyday people. Now, after more than 125 years of publishing and ministry, Moody Publishers' mission remains the same—even if our delivery systems have changed a bit. For more information on other books (and resources) created from a biblical perspective, go to www.moodypublishers.com or write to:

Moody Publishers
820 N. LaSalle Boulevard
Chicago, IL 60610

1 3 5 7 9 10 8 6 4 2

Printed in the United States of America

CONTENTS

For Sam,
my brother and my friend,
without whose encouragement
I would probably have given up on this book.

INTRODUCTION

"Are you crying?"

It was two weeks before I planned to start this book, and I was trying to plug my phone into an outlet in our church office when my friend Lexi walked in. I almost never cry in front of people. For a moment, I considered saying, "No." But after a pause, I mumbled, "Yes." I'd just submitted final edits on another book, and that had kept me going for the morning. But after pressing send, I found myself just sitting with my feelings, and they were not good.

Two days earlier, I'd given a mediocre talk for the ministry of a dear friend. I felt like I'd let her down and it was haunting me and causing me to question if she'd still want to be close. The day before, a dear non-Christian friend of many years had told me she was questioning whether we could still be friends, given our deep ideological differences. I've always battled fear around close friendships, waiting for the day my friends would realize they didn't want me anymore. In the two years prior to that week, I'd made substantial progress in fighting insecurity. But now the time had come to write this book, and I was having a resurgence of old friendship fears. I stammered out some pieces of this narrative to Lexi. She looked me in the eye and said, "I could spend time reassuring you that your talk was probably better than you think. But I know the relational stuff is what you really care about. So instead, I'm going to tell you quite how much your friendship means to me."

There are many times in the Bible when God sends one person to another with a message. Seldom in my life have I felt more like God sent someone to me. This particular friend, and the particular things she said to me that morning, made it just as clear that God was holding me as if He'd etched it in the sky. Neither Lexi nor I had planned that conversation. If I had known she was walking up the stairs, I would have bitten back my tears. What's more, the night before, she'd told her husband everything she said to me, and even that convergence made me feel God's care. I thoroughly believe that God directs my life, but rarely does He let me see the script. That moment was a picture of a precious gift the Lord gives to His people: friends, who help us up when we have hit the ground. But there's a catch.

That day in the church office, God dispatched a friend to help me in the tenderness that I was feeling from two other friends. Friend help was sent to salve friend hurt. So, is friendship like some scratch-card offer where you pay up again and again because one card in twenty pays you back? Would we be better off withdrawing from the field of friendship, bandaging our wounds, and saying to ourselves, "I've learned my lesson and I'll never risk my heart with friends again"? I don't think so. In fact, if you, like me, are a follower of Jesus, I don't believe we have that option.

This book is not a memoir. I've made all the friendship mistakes in the book, and I could vomit out a volume of those stories. Slowly, tenderly, with many stumbles on the way, I think I've learned to better navigate the contours of this glorious and hazardous gift called friendship. God has blessed me with some truly faithful friends and taught me how to hold them close without engaging in the stranglehold that suffocates connection over time.

But rather than just recounting all my forays into friendship, this book explores the biblical terrain in which all Christian friendships set up camp. My claim is not that friendship is the only camper in this space. Many of the Scriptures we'll be mining will have implications for a range of other human bonds as well. But all the Scriptures we'll explore are relevant to Christian friendship and must shape how followers of Jesus think about this kind of love.

To navigate our friendships well, we need to map out where green pastures lie and chart the cracks and crevices—from the fear of closeness that can hold us back from forging real friendships to codependency, which turns a friendship in upon itself. We'll look at friendship challenges and opportunities for married people and for single people, for those of us who (like me) experience same-sex attraction, and for those attracted to the opposite sex. We'll spend some time on opportunities for male-female friendship, and we'll examine friendship between Christians and non-Christians. We'll see how friendship finds its place within the range of other bonds, and how it blesses all of us: male or female, married or single, hurting or happy, aging or young.

Friend is an elastic term. It stretches out one arm to grab acquaintances, while with the other it grasps onto those who know our darkest secrets and most vulnerable dreams. While this book will focus on the texture of close friendship, I want to hold space for the incidental kind. Like a conductor with an orchestra, we don't just need the first and second violin. We also need the triangle, which chimes in at the perfect time. But rather than assuming we're the center of the story, we must recognize that every member of our orchestra is also a conductor, and the piece each one of us is trying to play is not our own: it's one composed for us by God Himself. He is the orchestrator and the only audience that matters in the end. Our role is not to gather friends around ourselves to meet our needs and play our compositions. Rather, we are called to join with Jesus' relational ensembles and pursue His re-creative mission in this world.

> Like a conductor with an orchestra, we don't just need the first and second violin. We also need the triangle, which chimes in at the perfect time.

In his influential book *The Four Loves*, Oxford scholar C. S. Lewis explored four different kinds of love through four Greek words. His chapter on *philia* or friendship love is the go-to resource for many Christians to this day. But while much of what Lewis writes is fruitful and provocative, his exposition of this kind of love is mostly drawn not from the Scriptures, but from classical paradigms of friendship and his own experience.

When it comes to a biblical grounding of deep friendship love, Christians have tended to look back to the Old Testament relationship between David and his much older brother-in-law Jonathan. After David's famous victory over Goliath, we're told that "the soul of Jonathan was knit to the soul of David, and Jonathan loved him as his own soul" (1 Sam. 18:1). Later, after Jonathan's death, David laments, "I am distressed for you, my brother Jonathan; very pleasant have you been to me; your love to me was extraordinary, surpassing the love of women" (2 Sam. 1:26). The fact that some contemporary commentators read romantic love into these statements goes to show how much we struggle to conceive of deeply precious nonromantic love.

But there are various ways in which David and Jonathan's relationship does not map straightforwardly onto friendship—including the political dimensions of their bond. Instead of anchoring on this Old Testament relationship, my hope in this book is to anchor our understanding of friendship on Jesus Himself, and the examples of deep Christian friendship that we find in the New Testament.

As we sit at Jesus' feet, we must be ready to have our assumptions about self-serving friendship shaken up. While having dinner at a Pharisee's house, Jesus gave His host some feedback on His future guest lists: "When you give a dinner or a banquet, do not invite your friends or your brothers or your relatives or rich neighbors, lest they also invite you in return and you be repaid. But when you give a feast, invite the poor, the crippled, the lame, the blind, and you will be blessed, because they cannot repay you" (Luke 14:12–14). Our aim if we are Christians must not be to form a club of peers who scratch our backs as we scratch theirs. We must be reaching out to welcome those in need. But Jesus also modeled deep investment in a few relationships, and the premise of this book is that the startling claim that Jesus made the night He was betrayed is true: "Greater love has no one than this, that someone lay down his life for his friends" (John 15:13).

For Christians, I will argue, friendship is no optional extra life feature we might get talked into by an eager salesman. It's vital to our flourishing. Friendship at its best is just as powerful as any other love. But like each one of God's amazing gifts to us, it's life-giving if we embrace it well, and soul-sucking if we don't.

Friendship can fuel and shape us in delightful, God-exalting ways, or it can hurl us headlong into sin.

> **Friendship is no optional extra life feature we might get talked into by an eager salesman. It's vital to our flourishing.**

Friendship can revive us when we're left for dead, or it can grind us down into the dust.

Friendship can project us forward in our following of Christ, or it can drag us back.

Unlike marriage, friendship is designed to incorporate variety and it can be experienced and enjoyed with a wide range of people who we know to varying degrees. But we will only gain the full goods of this gift if we are also ready for the risk and vulnerability of opening our hearts and lives up to a smaller number of mutually invested friends.

If you are not a Christian, my hope is that this book will help you grow in friendship. But I also hope that you will see how friendship is a pointer to an even greater love: the love that Jesus showed to you when He laid down his life two thousand years ago. If Christianity is true, then any joy, delight, and comfort we might find in friends is just an echo of that greater love. While other friends will never ultimately satisfy, the one Friend who has loved us to the point of an excruciating death is also ready and equipped to walk us through our own death into everlasting life—if we will only let Him take our hand.

If you are a Christian, I hope this book will help you grow more durable, missional, challenging, comforting, life-giving friendships. If Jesus is right that there is no greater love than to lay down our lives for our friends, we need to learn this love as if our life depends on it. We need to form deep friendships, so that we can fight the battles Jesus calls us to with comrades by our sides. We need them there to brace us for the onslaught, stoke our joy, and celebrate the victories along the way. But we also need our friends, so that when we slump down under the weight of all our frailty and failure, there will be someone there to ask us, "Are you crying?" and we'll have the courage to say, "Yes."

chapter one

NO GREATER LOVE

My friend Yashar was born in the Islamic Republic of Iran.[1] But Islam never won his heart. Like many of his fellow countrymen, Yashar experienced the disillusionment that comes from forced religious practices. When Yashar's family moved to Turkey, he continued to be surrounded by Islam, though his family and most of his friends were not religious. But while he was in Istanbul, a fellow Iranian started talking to him about Jesus. Yashar was not convinced. However, he decided to read John's gospel to find out more about Jesus and to assure himself that Christianity was just as uncompelling as Islam. "The verse that got me was John 15:13," Yashar recalls, "when Jesus says to His disciples, 'Greater love has no one than this: that he lay down his life for his friends.' I'd been searching for the true definition of love," Yashar told me. "But friends and girlfriends and family hadn't satisfied my longing. I knew that in Jesus I had found the definition and the source of love."

In this chapter, I want to start our exploration of what Christian friendship looks like, how important it can be, and how embedded Christian friendship is not in our natural reserves of love for one another, but in Jesus' supernatural love for us. My hope in these next pages is to excavate the gospel shape of Christian friendship, and to demonstrate how tethered to the death and life of Jesus it must be if we're to feast on its delights. You see, in Christian friendship, we can get a glimpse of Jesus' precious love for us: the love that wooed Yashar from death to everlasting life. But if we are to grasp the gospel message at the heart of Christian friendship, we need to grasp the insufficiency of every friendship we will ever have before we meet with Jesus face-to-face.

RESUME OF FAILURE

In 2010, Caltech postdoc Melanie Stefan published an article in the leading science journal, *Nature*. The article was titled "A CV of Failures." The lede read, "Keeping a visible record of your rejected applications can help others to deal with setbacks."[2] Six years later, Princeton professor Johannes Haushofer made his own "CV of failures" public. It went viral. He dutifully added a line:

> This darn CV of Failures has received way more attention than my entire body of academic work.[3]

For most of us, our record of relationships is just as carefully curated as our resume. But if your life has been like mine, you could easily bang out a resume of friendship failure. The friend you lost. The friend you tried to gain but never got. The friend who ghosted you. The friend you wanted to be close to but who kept you at arm's length. The friend you trusted with your secrets but who shared them out like donuts.

Perhaps, through all this failure, you have learned to manage life without the kind of friends who know your weaknesses and fears. You've learned the hard way that it's safer not to trust. Perhaps, despite some disappointments, you have had enough success at friendship that you've carried on. Or maybe all this talk of friendship love feels alien—like people getting all worked up about a sport you've never played. Perhaps the notion of a tragic friendship loss sounds like we're back in middle school. Those of us who still care deeply about friendship can feel a little sheepish. But the devaluing of friendship love is not how things have always been.

"To the Ancients," C. S. Lewis observed, "Friendship seemed the happiest and most fully human of all loves; the crown of life and the school of virtue."[4] In the fourth century BC, the Greek philosopher Aristotle stated bluntly that "without friends no one would choose to live, though he had all other goods."[5] Aristotle famously put friendship in three categories: friendships of pleasure, of utility, and of virtue.[6] In today's terms, we might see the first as friendships built around shared interests; the second as networking; and the third as friendships we invest in in a deeper sense—ones in which each person seeks the other's good and recognizes the goodness in the other as they seek to grow in goodness side by side. Many in our society today have friends of pleasure or utility; fewer have friends of virtue. These relationships take much more serious investment.

Noticing the gap between what ancient authors wrote and how his British contemporaries thought, Lewis described a common perception of friendship as "something quite marginal; not a main course in life's banquet; a diversion; something that fills up the chinks of one's time." How has this devaluation of the currency of friendship come about? "The first and most obvious answer," Lewis suggests, "is that few value [friendship] because few experience it."[7] So, what might friendship look like at its best?

Interned in a Nazi prison the year before his execution, German theologian Dietrich Bonhoeffer wrote a poem titled "The Friend." Inspired by his best friend, Bonhoeffer describes the unique nature of friendship compared to other loves like this:

> not from the heavy soil of earth
> but from the heart's free choosing
> and from the spirit's free longing
> needing no oath or legal sanction
> is the friend given to the friend

As we'll see in chapter 7, there's something about freedom that gives friendship its uniquely vital quality. But friendship isn't just a place of freedom. It is also a domain of comfort, refreshment, safety, and delight. Bonhoeffer goes on:

> Like a clear, fresh wellspring
> where the spirit cleanses itself from the day's dust,
> where it cools itself after blazing heat
> and steels itself in the hour of fatigue—

Like a fortress, where the spirit returns
after confusion and danger,
finding refuge, comfort, and strength,
such is the friend to the friend.[8]

Bonhoeffer profoundly treasured friendship love. But he was no fresh-faced idealist. As we'll see in chapter 2, Christian friendship grows within the broader scope of Christian fellowship, and of this fellowship, Bonhoeffer wrote, "Just as surely as God desires to lead us to a knowledge of genuine Christian fellowship, so surely must we be overwhelmed by a great disillusionment with others, with Christians in general, and, if we are fortunate, with ourselves."[9]

Our resume of failure may seem like compelling evidence we shouldn't try again with friendship love. But if Bonhoeffer is right, it could be our best starting point. And when we look at Jesus' famous words on friendship love, we'll find that they're delivered when He knew He was about to be betrayed, denied, abandoned by His closest friends.

A NEW COMMANDMENT

Judas, one of Jesus' twelve chosen apostles, had just walked out into the night when Jesus turned to His remaining followers and gave them these astounding marching orders:

"A new commandment I give you, that you love one another: just as I have loved you, you also are to love one another. By this all people will know that you are my disciples, if you have love for one another." (John 13:34–35)

Love had been the pounding heart of Jesus' ethical teaching—love of God, love of neighbor, even love of enemies. So, how was this commandment new? The newness of His words is anchored in what Jesus was about to do. On that dark night, He called His followers to plunge themselves deeper into love than they had ever gone, because their love for one another was to be *just like* His love for them. This love was set up as the hallmark of discipleship.

Earlier that evening, Jesus had given them a model of self-sacrificing love. He'd stripped down to a towel around His waist and taken on the slave-associated role of washing His disciples' feet. He'd told them they should do the same for one another (John 13:1–15). His followers were likely still in shock. But this was just the prelude. They were soon to witness quite how far His love would go. When Jesus told His friends that they must love each other just like He loved them, He knew He was mere hours from the cross. He also knew that very night they would let Him down.

Peter was by any measure one of Jesus' closest friends. When Jesus took a subset of disciples with Him, Peter was always one of the three. Peter was, therefore, especially distressed when Jesus said that He was going somewhere His disciples could not yet follow. Peter replied, "Lord, why can I not follow you now? I will lay down my life for you" (John 13:37). Jesus responded, "Will you lay down your life for me? Truly, truly I say to you, the rooster will not crow till you have denied me three times" (v. 38). Jesus was right. That night, with Jesus' call to love still ringing in his ears, Peter denied three times he even knew his Lord.

Peter's claim that he would "lay down [his] life" for Jesus, and Jesus' devastating prophecy to the contrary, are hanging in the air when Jesus uses the language of life laid down the second time:

> "This is my commandment, that you love one another as I
> have loved you. Greater love has no one than this, that some-
> one lay down his life for his friends." (John 15:12–13)

I've read these words a hundred times, but I'm only gradually
waking up to what they mean. Jesus summons His divine authority to give us this commandment. He is the one who has the right
to order us: He made us, and our every breath depends on Him.
What's more, He has the *might* to order us: He is the one who can
stop storms by speaking to the wind and sea (Mark 4:41). If even
storms obey Him, how much more must we weak creatures bend to
Jesus' commandments? But Jesus in this moment doesn't summon
us to do His bidding on the grounds that He created us, or on the
grounds that He could force us to comply. No. He commands His
followers (both then and now) on the authority of His hell-break-
ing love. His rule over His followers is not just "loving rule," as if
it could have taken on a different adjective. It is the rule of love
itself: love written in His blood. So, what does Jesus mean when He
applies this rule to friendship?

WHAT DOES "FRIEND" MEAN?

In the New Testament, the Greek word most frequently translated
"friend" is *philos*. Jesus' words account for eighteen of its twenty-
nine instances. He uses the term most often in His teachings (e.g.,
Luke 15:9). But Jesus also uses *philos* to describe His own relationships: calling His disciples "my friends" (Luke 12:4; John 15:14) and

quoting critics calling Him "a friend of tax collectors and sinners" (Luke 7:34). In the Gospels, *philos* usually describes connection between peers: for instance, when King Herod and the Roman governor Pilate become friends in the process of condemning Jesus (Luke 23:12).[10] But against our modern expectations, *philos* could also be used to describe hierarchical relationships: for instance, when those trying to get Jesus crucified tell Pilate he's no friend of Caesar's if he doesn't find Jesus guilty (John 19:12). In fact, as Daniel Eng has pointed out, *philos* was frequently used to describe the client in Greco-Roman patron-client relationships, which were intrinsically unequal: "The oldest and most persistent patron-client relationships existed between a former master and his freedman...." Eng explains. "By granting freedom, the former master became a patron and could expect to receive honor and pledged loyalty from his clients."[11]

This context helps illuminate the next words out of Jesus' mouth after He says that there's no greater love than laying down one's life for one's friends:

> "You are my friends if you do what I command you. No longer do I call you servants, for the servant does not know what his master is doing; but I have called you friends, for all that I have heard from my Father I have made known to you." (John 15:14–15)

In Jesus' sacrificial love, we see a radical reversal. The one who is our rightful master lays His life down for those who by all rights should be His servants. Jesus is the master, patron, teacher—and yet He came "not to be served but to serve, and to give his life as a ransom for many" (Mark 10:45). But this revolutionary flipping of the patron-client bond is not all that Jesus has in mind. John's gospel also gives us evidence that Jesus shared in friendship with His followers in another, more familiar sense.

In John 11, Mary and Martha of Bethany call for Jesus because their brother, Lazarus, is sick. Jesus waits until Lazarus is dead before He sets off. Then He says to His disciples, "Our friend Lazarus has fallen asleep, but I go to awaken him" (John 11:11). Jesus doesn't say "my friend," but "our friend." This indicates that Jesus did not only use *philos* in the patron-client sense when He applied it to His own relationships. While Lazarus could be His *philos* in that sense, he wouldn't have that patron-client bond with Jesus' other followers. It also suggests that *philos* was a term used by His followers to capture their relationships with one another. Lazarus' friendship with Jesus' itinerant disciples evidently ran deep. Thomas responds to the news of Lazarus' death by saying to the others, "Let us also go, that we may die with him" (John 11:16). So, how does all this context help us understand what Jesus' words on friendship love might mean for us?

HOW DOES JESUS' COMMANDMENT IMPACT FRIENDSHIP?

Jesus' disciples did not choose to follow Him because they thought they'd fit in with His other friends. Rather, Jesus chose them. Their life together was contingent on relationship with Him, not first and foremost with each other. There's zero chance that Matthew the tax collector and Simon the Zealot would have selected one another on a friend connection app, or that Mary Magdalene, from whom Jesus had cast out seven demons, and Joanna the wife of Chuza, who had left King Herod's court to travel around with Jesus, would have been close friends in any other context (Luke 8:1–3). When Jesus calls His followers to love each other just like He loves them, He's not just going with the grain of natural friendship. He is calling people who might never have gone near each other into sacrificial-love relationships. Likewise, we should be ready to form Christian friendships with those utterly unlike us. And while sacrificial love is most associated in our minds with marriage and parenting, we need to recognize that Jesus issued His command to one-another love in the first instance to people who were one another's friends.

Jesus' linking of deep friendship love to His own sacrifice for us means friendship is a vehicle of the gospel, not just because in friendship we speak gospel truth to one another (though we should), nor even just because we seek to speak the truth of the gospel to friends who don't yet follow Jesus (though we must). Friendship is a vehicle for the gospel in the sense that its cross-shaped: formed for life laid down in love for others, just as Jesus laid down His own life for us. While Christian friendship can encompass more occasional connections, and the regular encouragement of seeing friends we mostly only see

> **Jesus issued His command to one-another love in the first instance to people who were one another's friends.**

at church, it must not be confined to such relationships. We must be ready for the blood and sweat and tears that come with every heart-arresting love. But friendship, as we'll see, is not designed to replicate the other kinds of human bond, but to complement them.

According to the Scriptures, the love we can experience in marriage, parent-child relationships, and friendship each shine lights on different aspects of God's love. The best love we could ever find in Christian marriage mimics how Christ loves His church (Eph. 5:25). The most devoted parent-child love gives us a glimpse of how the Father loves the Son—a love that Jesus tells us is extended to His followers (John 15:9). Likewise, the sweetest, sacrificial friendship love resembles how our Savior loves all those who put their trust in Him (John 15:12–13).

In modern Western culture, we are primed to think of friendship as a nice-to-have, while sexual and romantic love and parent-child love are vital to our thriving. But Jesus flips this script. Instead of telling His disciples that they must get married and have children, Jesus tells His followers that they must love each other, even to the point of death. When Jesus said there was no greater love than laying down one's life for one's friends, He wasn't being hyperbolic or naïve. Instead, He was inscribing the good news of His unfathomable love for us onto Christian friendship with indelible ink.

Before He left the table, Jesus rammed the point home one last time: "These things I command you, so that you will love one another" (John 15:17). Jesus' disciples were sent out with the message of His great, self-sacrificing love for sinners. They were to shout it from the rooftops. But they were also to embody it in how they loved each other. If we are followers of Jesus, one way we will demonstrate our love for Him is by our love for one another. But Jesus never said this would be easy.

WEAKNESS, DENIAL, AND BETRAYAL

After dinner, Jesus led His disciples to the garden of Gethsemane, where He told most of them to sit and wait. But then, despite what He had just predicted about Peter's failure, He picked Peter, James, and John to watch with Him, while He went further on to pray. These three had been with Jesus when He raised a twelve-year-old girl from the dead, and when He was revealed in His glory on a mountaintop. They were apparently His inner ring. And yet, when Jesus came back from pleading with His Father for the cup to pass from Him, He found them fast asleep. Hours earlier, Peter had claimed that he would die with Jesus. Now Jesus asks him, "Could you not watch with me one hour?" (Matt. 26:40). This cycle happened two more times. These were friends for whom Jesus was about to lay down His life. Yet they couldn't even stay awake one hour with Him. "The spirit indeed is willing," Jesus observed, "but the flesh is weak" (v. 41). Then, Judas came.

Judas had given those commissioned to arrest Jesus a sign: "The one I kiss is the man; seize him" (Matt. 26:48). So, he came to Jesus saying, "Greetings, Rabbi," and he kissed him (v. 49). Jesus answered, "Friend, do what you came to do" (v. 50). Strikingly, the word that Jesus uses is not *philos* but *hetairos*, which communicates a less intimate form of friendship: more like a comrade or companion.[12] Judas had spent a lot of time with Jesus. But he hadn't given Him his heart. This is a picture of false friendship.

Even before he sold Jesus out, Judas had been stealing from the common money bag (John 12:6).

Of course, Jesus' relationships with His disciples can't be neatly mapped onto our friendships. But just as He commanded His first followers to love one another like He loved them, so He commands His followers today to emulate that love. It's a love prepared to die for one's friends, despite their failure. It's a love that lives vulnerably even toward those false friends who may be finally exposed as only wanting to be with us for what they can get. It's a love that does not easily give up on friends who let us down, because the greatest friend of sinners has not given up on us.

Just as Jesus had predicted, Peter denied he knew his Lord three times. When Peter realized what he'd done, he wept bitterly (Matt. 26:75). Doubtless Peter thought this was the end for his relationship with Jesus. But Jesus had another plan. In one of their post-resurrection meetings, Jesus asked Peter a painful question: "Simon, son of John, do you love me more than these?" (John 21:15). Peter had thought that he was better than his comrades. When Jesus had predicted that each one of His disciples would fall away, Peter had replied, "Even though they all fall away, I will not" (Mark 14:29).

> It's a love that does not easily give up on friends who let us down, because the greatest friend of sinners has not given up on us.

Now, Peter simply responded to Jesus' question, "Yes, Lord; you know that I love you." Instead of pointing back to Peter's failure, Jesus pointed forward to his role: "Feed my lambs" (John 21:15). Then Jesus asked a second time, "Simon, son of John, do you love me?" Peter replied, "Yes, Lord; you know that I love you." And Jesus said to him, "Tend my sheep." (v. 16). As if to match the number of times Peter had denied him, Jesus asked a third time: "Simon, son of John, do you love me?" Peter was grieved because Jesus said to him the third time, "Do you love me?" But this time, instead of thinking he knew better than his Lord, Peter recognized that Jesus knew him better than he knew himself: "Lord, you know everything," Peter replied, "you know that I love you." Jesus said to him, "Feed my sheep" (v. 17).

In this remarkable exchange, we see the power of forgiveness. Jesus knew that Peter was a sinner from the first, and when we risk deep friendship with each other, we will find ourselves confronted with each other's sin. But Jesus' words of friendship love were spoken in full knowledge of Peter's denial, and the cowardice of the other disciples, who fled when Jesus was arrested. We could imagine Jesus wiping the slate clean and picking up another twelve apostles after He had risen from the dead. But while Judas permanently breaks the bond, we find that Jesus sticks with all the others who had left him. Jesus' confidence in resurrection life enabled Him to lay His own life down for His most undeserving friends. If we are friends of Jesus now, that same resurrection life flows through our veins and calls us to self-sacrificing love for one another. As my friend Yashar discovered, no one has greater love than Jesus. But we can emulate that love as we relate to one another. No. Scrap that. We must.

chapter two

NONTRADITIONAL FAMILY

I woke one summer Sunday morning feeling ready for the day. I knew that church was going to be a lot. Friends from England were visiting and needed to be hosted. A family we'd met at a church backpack giveaway the day before had said they'd like to come to church, so I was looking out for them. I wanted to meet the boyfriend of a woman in our community group, to welcome another woman who had just started coming to church after leaving an abusive relationship, to check in with a friend who was struggling with anxiety, and to see another friend who was dying of cancer. There were many items on my list that Sunday morning, but I thought I was ready. Reader, I was not ready.

Halfway through the service, someone tapped me on the shoulder to inform me that my husband, Bryan, was downstairs about to pass out. As I scurried out of the service, I asked Yashar, who is a doctor, to come with me. Yashar thought Bryan should be taken to urgent care, so I asked my friend Paige if she could take Yashar and Bryan to the doctor, while I took our kids home. Minutes after they arrived at urgent care, Bryan was rushed to the ER. So, Paige and Yashar came home to babysit while I went to the hospital. Bryan was on a cardiac ward for six days. What we experienced that week put flesh on the bones of the passage that was being preached that Sunday morning: a passage in which Jesus redefines the family.

It may seem odd to spend a chapter of a friendship book on church as family. But healthy Christian friendship grows on the trellis of Christian family love, so we need to get that scaffolding in place before we can explore the friendship vine.

FAMILY VALUES

One day, Jesus was teaching when His mother and brothers showed up. If anyone had the right to interrupt Jesus, you'd think it would be His mother. But instead of saying, "Family first: I'm out of here," Jesus asks, "Who is my mother, and who are my brothers?" Then, pointing to His followers, Jesus declares, "Here are my mother and my brothers! For whoever does the will of my Father in heaven is my brother and sister and mother" (Matt. 12:48–50). For Christians, family does come first. But it's the family of faith, not of biology.

Perhaps you're thinking, "Wait, aren't Christians known for *family values*, a strong prioritizing of marriage and kids?" Yes, Jesus had such a high view of marriage that even His disciples were shocked (Matt. 19:1–11). What's more, His welcoming of children and infants radically raised their value in the context of a Greco-Roman culture in which children were seen as possessions and babies were often abandoned (Matt. 19:13–15; Luke 18:15–17). Jesus is the reason for our valuing of marriage as a permanent, equal, and exclusive bond between a husband and a wife—and for our valuing of babies as persons in their own right. But Jesus didn't elevate the nuclear family above all else. The family He valued most was the family of His followers.

Right after Jesus validated little kids, a rich young ruler asked him, "Good Teacher, what must I do to inherit eternal life?" (Luke 18:18; see also Matt. 19:16; Mark 10:17). Jesus pointed him to God's commandments. Then He told the man to give all he had to the poor, and come and follow Him (Luke 18:22; see also Matt. 19:21; Mark 10:21). The man left sad. Jesus observed that it's harder for a rich man to enter God's kingdom than for a camel to go through the eye of a needle. Peter gushed, "We have left our homes and followed you." Jesus responded, "Truly, I say to you, there is no one who has left house or wife or brothers or parents or children, for the sake of the kingdom of God, who will

> Jesus didn't elevate the nuclear family above all else. The family He valued most was the family of His followers.

not receive many times more in this time, and in the age to come eternal life" (Luke 18:28–30; see also Matt. 19:29; Mark 10:28–30).

The biological family is a precious gift from God. But it's a gift that calcifies when cut off from the family of church. If we must choose between family and faithfulness to Jesus, we must choose Jesus. If following Jesus means we get rejected by our parents, remain single when we longed to marry, or miss out on having children, Jesus promises us much more in Christian family than we might have lost. For those who put their trust in Jesus, family does not come first. Jesus comes first. Our love for anyone and anything must stem from our first love for Him.

Earlier in Luke, Jesus voices the priority of loving Him above all others in offensive terms: "If anyone comes to me and does not hate his own father and mother and wife and children and brothers and sisters, yes, and even his own life, he cannot be my disciple" (Luke 14:26). The call is not literally to hate our families. As we've seen, Jesus insists on the unbreakable bond of marriage and the valuing of children. He calls the Pharisees hypocrites for breaking the fifth commandment by failing to provide for their parents (Mark 7:9–13). But we must nonetheless feel the force of Jesus' hyperbole: any love we have for human family should be *as nothing* when compared to how we love Him. Does this mean we cast family by the wayside as worthless? No. When we put love of Jesus first, we'll find we love our biological families more. Our love for them will be profoundly shaped by our love for Him, and when we live as if the local church is our true family, our biological families will benefit.

The week that Bryan was in the hospital, our kids were wrapped up in the love of our church family. Our friends who don't have kids did dance routines and crafts with them. Our friends who do have kids took them for playdates and sleepovers. Paige offered to take two days off work to care for them—an offer I declined, because we had the help we needed, but one that deeply touched my heart. One day that week, my friend Julia texted me to ask, "What's the plan for our kids today?" By saying "our" instead of "your" she made a point: our church friends were our family that week. Or rather, I should say, they *are* our family.

> When we put love of Jesus first, we'll find we love our biological families more. Our love for them will be profoundly shaped by our love for Him.

That week was just an opportunity to show it.

My friend Rachel and her husband, Andrew, took care of my kids for several days. I'd come home from the hospital knowing I needed to keep it together for my children's sake. But Rachel was aware how hard it was on my heart to see my husband's heart hooked up to monitors. In moments when the kids were occupied, she'd wrap her arms around me as a silent testament to how she knew I felt. Rachel's daughter commented that it was like my daughter Eliza was her sister that week. "She is," I replied. You see, the church is not just *like* a family. It *is* a family. Our first identity as followers of Jesus is not biological. It's theological.

THE OG NONTRADITIONAL FAMILY

One of Rachel's roles in my life is explaining popular culture. In case you're as uncool as I am, let me define OG for you, like Rachel did for me: it stands for "Original Gangster," and it means the first and perhaps finest. Despite my ignorance of popular expressions, even I'm familiar with "nontraditional family." This term applies to families that aren't just standard issue: single parent families; those built around a same-sex couple; "blended families," where kids from previous relationships are mixed; and even "chosen family"—a group of friends who see each other as their true family. In contrast to these "nontraditional" families, Christians are often seen as champions of traditional family. But this is only half the truth, because the church is the OG nontraditional family.

In the New Testament, the Greek word *adelphoi* is used over two hundred times to refer to siblings in Christ. Like "guys" in modern English, *adelphoi* is inclusive and can be translated "brothers" or "brothers and sisters." Sibling language is also applied to individuals. For instance, in his letter to the Romans, Paul references, "our sister Phoebe" (Rom. 16:1) and "our brother Quartus" (Rom. 16:23).

We modern Westerners are primed to look primarily to marriage and to parent-child relationships for our deepest commitment and emotional connection. But as New Testament professor Joseph Hellerman observes, for the New Testament's first readers, "marriage took a back seat priority-wise to another more important family relationship—the bond between blood brothers and sisters."[1] If forced to choose between their siblings and their spouse, they would be expected to choose their siblings. For them, brother-sister language was not sentimental fluff. It was quite serious.

Parent-child relationships were also fostered in the church. Paul greets "Rufus, chosen in the Lord; also his mother, who has been a mother to me as well" (Rom. 16:13). Conversely, he calls Timothy "my beloved and faithful child in the Lord" (1 Cor. 4:17), and Onesimus "my child" (Philem. 10). The message in a host of texts is clear: the church is family.

In the West, we pride ourselves on thinking individually, but the cultures within which the New Testament writings first circulated were ones in which the needs of the whole group were primary. In our culture, while someone might just sacrifice him- or herself for nuclear family, we remain enthralled by films and books that glamorize protagonists who choose their own romantic satisfaction over their spouse and kids. For us, the thinking of "strong-group societies"—where individuals believe not that their needs come first, but that their larger tribe should take priority—feels like a foreign language.

Our culture's message is quite clear: "Don't sacrifice your dreams or sexual fulfilment for anyone." This mantra would have been anathema to the first readers of the Gospels. Group thinking would have been more intuitive for them. But they would have been shocked by Jesus' call to trade in their first loyalty to their family of origin and sign up with the family of church.

We feel resistant to the church-as-family idea not only because it cuts against our individualism, but also because it's been abused. Just like a biological family, church family can be a setting for emotional and physical abuse. Just like in biological families, abuse in church families has all too often been sinfully enabled and covered up. What's more, too many cults and churches have been formed around impressive personalities and forced their members to relinquish ties with family to give their full allegiance to their leaders. None of this is biblical. Indeed, the apostle Paul specifically refuses to become the focus of the loyalty of followers of Jesus. "Was Paul crucified for you?" he asks the Corinthian Christians. "Were you baptized in the name of Paul?" (1 Cor. 1:13).

> **Just as all the evidence that biological families can be unhealthy and abusive doesn't lead us to give up on biological families, so examples of unhealthy churches should not lead us to give up on church as family.**

The only leader who deserves our total loyalty is the Master who was crucified for us, and we must recognize the capacity of any other human leader to sin. This means we must diversify the power in our churches and prioritize character over charisma in leaders (see Titus 1:5–9). But just as all the evidence that biological families can be unhealthy and abusive doesn't lead us to give up on biological families, so examples of unhealthy churches should not lead us to give up on church as family.

In Acts, after recording that three thousand people joined the church when God poured out His Spirit on His followers, Luke paints a stunning picture of the family behavior:

All who believed were together and had all things in common. And they were selling their possessions and belongings and distributing the proceeds to all, as they had need. And day by day, attending the temple together and breaking bread in their homes, they received their food with glad and generous hearts. (Acts 2:44–46)

Three thousand people can't live in one house. But these first Christians did their best to share, and they were clearly in and out of one another's homes. The week when Bryan was in the hospital, our Christian family stepped in to fill the need. This kind of sharing should increasingly become our norm if we are serious about the Scriptures.

I recently connected with a single mother at our church. She's working hard to raise her two young kids, and when her car broke down, she asked if I would pray. She didn't have the money set aside to get it fixed. I said I'd certainly be glad to pray. I also told her that our church has funds for needs like this. She was amazed. "I'm not used to people helping me and my kids," she said. I pointed out that since she'd started coming to our church, we are her family: it's our job to help.

The fact is, we will all need help at times. Perhaps we'll need financial help. Perhaps we'll need an errand run, a place to stay, someone to watch our kids, or start our car, or drive us to the hospital. Or maybe, we'll just need a listening ear, and arms around us while we sob. In any case, our church should be the place where we first turn when we need help—and it should be the place where we first look for needs that we can meet.

This paradigm of church as family must impact how we think about our Sunday gatherings, how we relate to marriage, how we engage in parenting, and how we pursue friendship. All these bonds belong and flourish in the family of church. Severed from this source, they risk becoming warped, shriveled, or bloated in unhealthy ways.

THE NUCLEAR OPTION

When Bryan and I want to flop down in front of something through which we can freely chat, we watch a nature documentary. This is how I know that cuckoo mothers lay their eggs in other species' nests. Worse, when the cuckoo hatches, it attempts to shove the other eggs out of the nest and to demand the parents of the murdered chicks feed it instead.

It struck me that, in many ways, our culture has let sexual and romantic love become the cuckoo chick: demanding all the nourishment at the expense of friendship and community. But while young cuckoos get built up on all this extra, stolen food, when we put all our focus on romantic love, we undermine it.

The longer I've been married, the more I am convinced that Christian marriage thrives when it's enfolded in the family of church. No marriage is an island. Not only do married believers, like me, need their siblings when their marriages are struggling, but we also need them in the normal times, especially when parenting.

My daughters have no Christian friends at school, and being a believer in a Cambridge, Massachusetts, public school today is rough. Our church is rich in under-ten-year-olds, but we have hardly any teens or tweens. Instead, my girls have adult friends who pour into their lives. Janice takes my twelve-year-old, Miranda, out for dinner and does baking projects with my ten-year-old, Eliza. Paige and Julia come by for chats and crafts and ice cream. Rachel kick-started Miranda on the discipline of daily Bible reading and meets with her to talk her studies through. Catherine takes the kids swimming, while Lou is teaching them to climb. The list goes on. These older siblings represent a range of ages, jobs, and circumstances. Through them, my children get to see the challenges and opportunities of different situations—including how to live a thriving, faithful, Christian life as a single person.

According to the Bible, singleness is just as valuable as marriage. In fact, Paul writes as if it's even better (1 Cor. 7:7). But in the modern, Western church,

> Singleness ought to be a rich and valued vehicle for discipleship. But we have treated it as a state that feels at best unenviable and at worst unlivable.

we've acted as if long-term singleness is either pitiable or selfish. In *The Meaning of Singleness*, Australian scholar Danielle Treweek points out that this hasn't always been the case. For centuries, most Christians thought of singleness as an elevated state, anticipating how we'll function in the new creation (Matt. 22:30). "Ironically and wonderfully," Treweek writes, "it is the unmarried form of life which most closely resembles the intrapersonal character of the heavenly bride!"[2] But current Christian norms too often marginalize or even stigmatize singleness. Singleness ought to be a rich and valued vehicle for discipleship. But we have treated it as a state that feels at best unenviable and at worst unlivable.

As someone with a lifelong history of same-sex attraction, I've written about the call for Christians to put Jesus first, not sexual fulfillment. People sometimes ask, "How can you expect people who are exclusively same-sex attracted to be lonely all their lives?" This question exposes a fundamental problem in our view of church. If marriage is the only refuge from loneliness for Christians, we are missing Jesus' call on all of us to be together in His mission. Sadly, this is often how we operate, even at our weekly gatherings.

EMERGENCY SERVICES

Each week, new people stumble into church alone. They may not yet be Christians, or they may be Christians looking for church family. Partly because of this, Bryan and I split up on Sundays to sit with newcomers, or people who have come alone. A few years back, I wrote an article explaining this: "Why I Don't Sit with My Husband at Church."[3] A glut of Christians took offense. How dare I undermine the family? How dare I think that people who come to church didn't want to sit alone? How dare I force my company on introverts? But at the same time, I received a flood of messages from single Christians sharing how much pain they felt in church because they sat alone.

If the church is family, we're not eroding family if spouses sometimes sit apart. We're building it. It's possible that someone new won't want to sit with you or me. But if they've come to church to be alone, they've come to the wrong place—like going to a restaurant with no appetite. We come to be together, not to have our private moment with the Lord. At some point, we will come to church with the deep need to grieve and not to talk. If so, let's grieve with others in companionable silence. But let's not leave each other lonely. In my experience, most people haven't come to church to be ignored, and many people don't come back to church because they tried it and they've felt alone.

Of course, we'll need to be attentive to the comfort of the other person. As a woman in my early forties, I enjoy the freedom that I have to sit with almost anyone and not be misinterpreted. If I were male, I'd avoid plumping myself down next to a young woman who had come to church for the first time. At times, we might spot someone new and tap another friend to sit with them. But everyone should feel the welcome of the church embodied in the individuals who seek them out.

To help us think through Sunday morning hospitality, Bryan has formulated three rules of engagement:

#1: An alone person in our gatherings is an emergency.

#2: Friends can wait.

#3: Introduce a newcomer to someone else.[4]

I love these principles and try to live by them. But often, as I've talked with other Christians, I've found that they're held back by undervaluing what they could offer other people. Last summer, for example, I had to tell a single sister (who is one of the most godly and delightful women I know) that by sitting alone at church, she's robbing others of the pleasures of her company. Tears filled her eyes. She worries she's infringing on the married folks if she sits next to them. While I am very sure that's not the case, I recognize that those of us who come to church with spouses have the primary responsibility to make our single siblings feel at home. In church, we married people have no right to act like we own the place. Rather, we together, single and married, *are* the place. Like army ants, which swarm 200,000 strong and form nests for their young with their own bodies, church should be an edifice of flesh and blood—built up as members cling to one another in formation to protect the vulnerable.

> He didn't just pull up a chair so we could sit; He picked up a cross, so we could live.

"Let each of us please his neighbor for his good, to build him up," Paul argues. "For Christ did not please himself, but as it is written, 'The reproaches of those who reproached you fell on me'" (Rom. 15:2–3). Imagine if we let this principle dictate how we behave in church! We wouldn't come to please ourselves, but rather to build each other up. Paul doesn't say that this is easy. In fact, he prays, "May the God of endurance and encouragement grant you to live in such harmony with one another, in accord with Christ Jesus, that together you may with one voice glorify the God and Father of our Lord Jesus Christ" (Rom. 15:5–6). We'll need endurance and encouragement from God to turn ourselves to one another's good. But we who have been welcomed by our Savior must extend that kind of welcome too. Paul concludes, "Therefore welcome one another as Christ has welcomed you, for the glory of God" (v. 7).

Jesus welcomed us in all our sin and weakness. He didn't just pull up a chair so we could sit; He picked up a cross, so we could live. Let's stretch and inconvenience ourselves on Sunday mornings to accommodate and welcome one another!

(UN)CHOSEN FAMILY

There's something so attractive about the sense of being chosen—picked out from the crowd—and there's a vital sense in which each local church should operate as chosen family. The problem is, we're not the ones who choose. Instead of picking one another out, we're stuck with Jesus' selections. This means church *isn't* like a chosen family of like-minded friends. Church family involves commitment to the people least like us—including those we may not even like. We'll find some members of our local church quite difficult. Perhaps they love the music that we hate. Perhaps they smell, or sing off-key, or voice political perspectives that we can't stand. We may want to turn away from them. But if they're members of our church, we can't. Instead, we need to move toward them, just as Jesus moved toward us.

As with our families of origin, this doesn't mean we should be forced into relationship with people who've abused us. There are times when boundaries must be put in place within the body of believers to allow one person to be kept away from someone else. There are also times when members of a church must fall under church discipline for unrepentant sin.[5] In cases like these, trusted leadership should care for and protect the injured party. Paul's point is not that every person in the church should be the one to welcome every other person. But everyone should be involved in the welcoming work of the church—just as everyone should be involved in helping those in need. We Christians are a family, and we must welcome those who join our gatherings as siblings.

Thankfully, the symptoms that got Bryan hospitalized last August turned out not to be a cause for serious concern. Instead, they were a cause for our church family to show love. I wasn't ready on that Sunday morning. But my spiritual family was. How is this relevant to deep, abiding, costly Christian friendship? Just as Christian biological family belongs in the broader family of church, so Christian friendship lives and thrives within the broader network of community. Just as biological family at its best strengthens the broader family of church, so Christian friendship at its best drives each of us to give ourselves more fully to the family of church. But if the followers of Jesus are called to love their whole church family, is there any role for more specific, focused, individual love in friendship? That's the question at the heart of chapter 3.

chapter three

MY VERY HEART

In her 2022 book, *Platonic*, psychologist Marisa Franco argues that as expectations around married love have grown in the West, and as same-sex romance has been normalized, the space for non-romantic friendship love has shrunk. As one manifestation of this change, Franco diagnoses "the jumbling of any type of love with sexual love," to the point where it can be hard for us to verbalize our love for friends. But even as she identifies this problem, Franco joins in with the jumbling: "At a time when love wasn't monopolized by spouses," she writes, "remnants of romance were apparent among famous friends of the past. Alexander Pope, the English poet, wrote to Jonathan Swift, the satirist, 'It is an honest truth, there's no one living or dead of whom I think oft'ner, or better than yourself.'"[1]

In this chapter, I want to argue that we must reclaim the language and the physical expression of deep friendship love, and that we don't need to requisition language of romantic love to talk about the passionate connection we might feel with friends—if we love being with them, go on about how wonderful they are, delight to wrap our arms around them, share our secrets with them, laugh loudly at their jokes, and miss them when they're not around. Instead, we'll see that there is ample precedent for full-blooded, nonromantic, deeply rooted friendship love in the New Testament.

THE DISCIPLES JESUS LOVED

Famously, the author of John's gospel never shares his name. Instead, he calls himself "the disciple Jesus loved" (John 13:23; 19:26; 20:2; 21:7, 20). The first time this title appears is shortly before Jesus' command of love, when he had just predicted His betrayal at the hands of one of the apostles. John writes:

> One of his disciples, whom Jesus loved, was reclining at table at Jesus' side, so Simon Peter motioned to him to ask Jesus of whom he was speaking. So that disciple, leaning back against Jesus, said to him, "Lord, who is it?" (John 13:23–25)

This moment of physical closeness, combined with John's description of himself, has led some commentators to conclude that Jesus was romantically involved with this disciple. But even if we only look at evidence from John's gospel itself, this theory is unsustainable.

Two chapters earlier, two of Jesus' female disciples, Mary and Martha, send Jesus a message: "Lord, he whom you love is ill" (John 11:3). They're not talking about John, but about their brother, Lazarus. In this instance, the verb translated "love" is *phileō*, not *agapaō*—the verb John tends to use when he calls himself the disciple Jesus loved.[2] But John uses *agapaō* to describe Jesus' love for Lazarus two verses later: "Now Jesus loved Martha and her sister and Lazarus" (John 11:5). John's intention when he calls himself "the disciple Jesus loved" cannot be to signal an exclusive or romantic love. Lazarus too was the one Jesus loved—and so are Mary and Martha, whose love-imbued relationships with Jesus are the focus of John 11:17–37 and 12:1–8. In brushstroke after brushstroke of John's gospel, we see Jesus' relationships with friends He loves so much He'll lay His life down for them.

The language of love in Jesus' relationships is not confined to His close friends. When Mark reports Jesus' encounter with the rich young man, he gives this detail: "Jesus, looking at him, loved him" (Mark 10:21). Like Jesus, we must act in love toward all those who come within our orbit: neighbor, colleague, stranger, friend, even enemy. But like Jesus, we must also share ongoing love with individuals with whom we spend extended time. We see this modeled helpfully by the apostle Paul.

MY VERY HEART

Paul starts his letter to Philemon with a string of epithets. He calls his coauthor "Timothy our brother," and addresses the letter to "Philemon our beloved fellow worker and Apphia our sister and Archippus our fellow soldier, and the church in your house" (Philem. 1–2). All these titles speak to warmth and intimacy. But Paul's most effusive language is reserved for the primary subject of the letter: Onesimus, who once lived as a bondservant in Philemon's household. I've written elsewhere about how this letter far from endorsing slavery radically undermines it.[3] Here, I want to focus on the relationship Paul evidently had with Onesimus.

Paul's purpose in writing this letter was to send Onesimus back to Philemon "no longer as a bondservant, but more than a bondservant, as a beloved brother—especially to me, but how much more to you" (Philem. 16). Paul expects Philemon to receive Onesimus not as member of his household staff, but as a brother, whom he loves. Paul shares his deep affection for Onesimus: "I appeal to you for my child, Onesimus," he writes, "whose father I became in my imprisonment" (v. 10).

The point of calling Onesimus "my child" is not to highlight a difference of age but to present Onesimus as Paul's heir: a status someone living under slavery could not achieve. Then Paul goes even further in his commendation: "I am sending him back to you, sending my very heart" (v. 12). The Greek word translated heart literally means bowels or intestines, which were seen as a place of deep emotion. Paul uses the same word later when he writes, "Yes, brother, I want some benefit from you in the Lord. Refresh my heart in Christ" (v. 20). Onesimus is Paul's very heart, and Paul calls Philemon to receive Onesimus as he would receive Paul himself (v. 17).

Paul's level of intense identification with Onesimus is how I feel about my closest friends. If you attack my friends, you'll deal with me. If you bless them, you're blessing me. I feel this way about my husband and my children. But I also feel this way about my friends. Rachel once told me she'd give all the money she had to keep me as her friend. It was a purely hypothetical remark. I wasn't needing money. She was just communicating love to me. I'd do the same for her. Likewise, Paul opened up his checkbook for Onesimus: "If he has wronged you at all, or owes you anything," Paul wrote, "charge that to my account" (Philem. 18). We should honor, protect, and provide for our friends. We should be unashamed to gush about how great they are and how much we love them. We should be prepared to back our words up with our finances. But unlike married love, this deep friendship love does not belong to just one other person.

Truth be told, I've always skimmed the greetings in Paul's letters. But as I've pondered on New Testament friendships, I've realized that what seem to us like random names are really records of ancient relationships. Paul's letter to the Romans ends with a laundry list of greetings. First, he commends the woman who likely delivered the letter: "Our sister Phoebe, a servant of the church at Cenchreae" (Rom. 16:1). Paul also calls her "a patron of many and of myself as well" (v. 2). The word translated "patron" is often translated as leader or ruler. Paul holds Phoebe in the highest respect and tells the Christians in Rome to "welcome her in the Lord in a way worthy of the saints, and help her in whatever she may need" (v. 2).

Paul then moves to a couple named Prisca (or Priscilla) and Aquila, of whom he says they "risked their necks for my life" (v. 4). This is a concrete instance of the "no greater love" that Jesus described to His disciples. Prisca and Aquila were willing to lay down their lives for Paul. But their commitment to him does not come from hours playing golf together. It springs from their shared mission: they are "fellow workers in Christ Jesus" (Rom. 16:3). In

Acts 18, we get a glimpse of their relationship. They met in Corinth and worked together practically as tentmakers (Acts 18:3). Next, they set sail for Syria together, following Jesus' continuing call to mission (v. 18). Priscilla and Aquila were Paul's co-laborers in every sense. In Aristotle's terms, they were friends of virtue.

Next up in Romans is Epaenetus, whom Paul calls "my beloved" (Rom. 16:5). Depending on your cultural background, this language may sound more or less intense. I come from England, where you could be really close to somebody for years and never say, "I love you." According to a 2021 survey, fewer than half of Americans (25 percent of men and 49 percent of women) had told a friend they loved them in the preceding week.[4] But Paul had zero problem expressing his love for the men with whom he had a close relationship. Epaenetus was Paul's beloved. But he was not the *only* man for whom Paul felt such affection. Paul also calls Ampliatus, "my beloved in the Lord," and sends greetings to "my beloved Stachys" (Rom. 16:8–9). If you're a Christian, you've every right to tell your friends you love them. In fact, there might be something wrong if there is no one you would want to speak to in that way.

Paul doesn't use the specific language of friendship in his greetings, but John does. He addresses his third recorded letter to "the beloved Gaius, whom I love in truth" (3 John 1), and then, after calling Gaius "beloved" three more times, he concludes, "I had much to write to you, but I would rather not write with pen and ink. I hope to see you soon, and we will talk face to face. Peace be to you. The friends greet you. Greet the friends, each by name" (3 John 13–15). While "brother" is a much more typical New Testament term for fellow believers, this ending indicates that first-century

Christians would also have described the members of their local church as friends.

If we are following the apostles' playbook, we should be expressing love to Christian friends. We should be unashamed to say we miss them when they're gone, as Paul did when he wrote to Timothy, "As I remember your tears, I long to see you, that I may be filled with joy" (2 Tim. 1:4). We should be ready to admit that losing them would break our heart, as Paul did when he told the Philippians that if Epaphroditus had died, he would have felt "sorrow upon sorrow" (Phil. 2:27). We are not trespassing on romance when we use such terms. We're following the Scriptures. What's more, we should be ready to express our friendship love with physical affection.

IN JESUS' BOSOM

Last night at our community group, people were squashed on couches and strewn on the floor. Three guys squeezed into a loveseat and Yashar casually draped his arm around Aahnix's shoulders. They stayed like that for much of the Bible study. In Iran, it's typical for men to put their arms around each other's shoulders, link arms, kiss each other on the cheek, and generally express their friendship with physical touch. In the United States, such physical connection is more typical of romantic relationships, but this has not always been the case.

Marisa Franco tells the story of Abraham Lincoln's emotionally and physically close friendship with his roommate Joshua Speed. She observes that, "In Lincoln's era, homosexuality was so squarely forbidden that intimacy between friends didn't raise concerns for its presence. This freed people to be as close to friends as they wished."[5] Today, Westerners effectively reserve extended physical connection for romantic or parental love. There's still some latitude for women. More elongated hugs to greet or say goodbye to friends are daily norms for me. But sitting with an arm around a female friend is on the border of what's acceptable for adult women in most Western contexts. It's fine if one of them is crying—otherwise not so much. Meanwhile, the fear of being misinterpreted has, as Franco puts it, "ravaged straight men's friendships."[6] For many men, sports are the only context in which they can be physically bonded with their friends in celebration or lament. Just casually sitting with an arm around a male friend while stone-cold sober at a Bible study would raise many Western eyebrows. But for followers of Jesus, it should not.

The author of John describes himself leaning against Jesus as they reclined at dinner (John 13:25). Literally, John was reclining on Jesus' chest or (in more archaic terms) bosom. In the standard, ancient Greek translation of the Old Testament, the same language describes the close connection between a husband and a wife (Deut. 13:6; 28:54, 56). But this language was not specifically sexual. At the beginning of John's gospel, the same expression describes the Son's intimacy with the Father: "No one has ever seen God; the only God, who is at the Father's side, he has made him known" (John 1:18). We also see it in Luke's gospel when Jesus tells a story about a rich man and a poor man named Lazarus. Both died. The rich man went to Hades, and the poor man was carried by angels to "Abraham's side" (Luke 16:22). Reclining on someone's chest communicates

intimacy and confers status. In our terms, it might translate as saying, "You're my intimate friend and right-hand man."

When Jesus said to His disciples, "A new commandant I give to
you, that you love one another: just as I have loved you, you also are
to love one another" (John 13:34), the author of John was likely still
lying in Jesus' arms. One way in which we can resemble Jesus in our
love for one another is by showing physical affection to our friends.

GREET ONE ANOTHER WITH A HOLY KISS

Poignantly, alongside Jesus' closeness with the author of John, the
other gospel evidence we have of Jesus' physical intimacy with His
disciples comes at the moment of Judas' betrayal. Luke records
Jesus' painful question: "Judas, would you betray the Son of Man
with a kiss?" (Luke 22:48). Judas kissing Jesus was a sign of their
friendship even as it became the signal of betrayal. But this did not
invalidate the kiss of fellowship for Christians.

In Acts, we see the elders of the church in Ephesus embracing
Paul, kissing him, and weeping over him as he departs, and they
know they will never see his face again (Acts 20:37). But this is
not a one-off flurry of affection. Three times, Paul urges believers
to "Greet one another with a holy kiss" (Rom. 16:16; 1 Cor. 16:20;
2 Cor. 13:12), and once, "Greet all the brothers with a holy kiss"
(1 Thess. 5:26). Likewise, Peter writes, "Greet one another with
the kiss of love" (1 Peter 5:14). Physical expressions of affection
between Christians should be part and parcel of our life together.

Of course, in different cultures, different kinds of physical
affection will be best received. One of the shifts I had to make

when I moved from the UK to the US was that whereas in the UK, it's normal for women to kiss both men and women on the cheek, in the US it's not. Conversely, British men are reticent to hug each other, whereas in the US hugs between men seem to be more common. We need to be attentive to our culture and the comfort of the other person as we think about our physical connection. But we should not let romantic love rob friendship of its physical expression. When we put our arms around our friends, we're telling them we love them in a tangible, biblical way. And yet, in the same epistles where we witness Paul's deep friend affection for the gospel partners whom he loves, we see another powerful dynamic at the heart of Christian friendship love: the willingness to send our friends away, if Jesus wills it so.

SENDING MY HEART

The first ten years I lived in Cambridge, Massachusetts, I lost half my friends each year. I hated it. The transientness of the city meant that people came and went continually. No sooner had I formed deep friendships, so it seemed, then they were ripped away. Ellen moved back to South Africa. Philippa moved to the Philippines. Sarah moved to New York. Janine moved to Canada. The grief of leaving those I loved in England was made more brutal by the loss of friendship after friendship over here.

Of course, in this strange age of digital connection, we can keep up friendships over distances in ways our forebears couldn't. But we also need embodied friendship. We need to hug and eat and walk and laugh with friends. But in Paul's letter to Philemon, we hear

Paul sending Onesimus—his very heart—away from him. Unlike the bond of marriage, friendship love is open to the possibility that we might need to send the friends, who are our very heart, away if they are called to follow Jesus in another place. We welcome friends with open arms and hold them with an open hand. The grief of parting, when it comes, is real. The elders of the church at Ephesus wept openly and hugged and kissed their brother Paul when he was sent away from them.

This openness to loss does not make friendship love a lesser kind of love. It cannot be, if we believe what Jesus said to His disciples. But it does make friendship love a different kind of love from married love. If Bryan moves to California one day, I'll move there too. If I moved back to England, he'd come with me. There may be seasons in which a married person must be separated from their spouse for weeks or months because of their profession (e.g., if someone in the military is deployed). But this should never be the norm. The one-flesh reality of marriage means that spouses should be in one home as their default. But there's a built-in flexibility to friendship love that must be ready for the possibility of change arising from location or life circumstances.

A range of factors might mean we fly in different friend formations as the years go by. Paul modeled this as he moved round the ancient world with different comrades, and we'll see this in our own lives, as we move or as our situations change. When I had my first child, I realized all my closest friends worked full-time jobs and I would need to find some friends who were available for daytime hangouts, as I now worked part-time. This did not mean that I lost my full-time working friends, but it did mean that I made space for new friends who were able to spend time with me on random afternoons.

Likewise, we might find that challenges in life require us to build new friendships: for example, with a person who will understand the grief of miscarriage, or who has walked through seasons of depression. The flexibility of friendship should not lead us to draw back from it or to have an easy come, easy go mentality. Rather, we should treasure what we have.

I thank the Lord continually for the dear friends He's given me close by. I get to interact with Christians I profoundly love week in and week out. But part of each of these relationships is knowing that—no matter how much we've invested in our friendship—one day, God could call us to serve Him in different places or in different ways. We are first and foremost fellow soldiers, and we'll go where we're deployed. But far from cramping our connection, this first allegiance to our Lord, who has the right to move us any time, stands at our connection's core. We're comrades in arms.

chapter four

COMRADES
IN ARMS

At the beginning of J. R. R. Tolkien's The Lord of the Rings, Sam is Frodo's gardener. Sam and Frodo are both hobbits: physically small and politically insignificant people among the inhabitants of Tolkien's "Middle-earth." But Frodo finds himself reluctantly entrusted with the task of destroying the evil ring of power, and Sam is recruited to go with him. At the beginning of the story, Sam calls his employer "Mr. Frodo." But halfway through their mission, Frodo calls Sam "Samwise Gamgee, my dear hobbit—indeed, Sam my dearest hobbit, friend of friends."[1] How has Sam gone from being Frodo's gardener to his "friend of friends"? Through months of facing danger side by side.

The closeness that builds up between these hobbits pictures Christian friendship at its best: fierce, committed comradeship around a mission that requires us to risk our lives. In this chapter, we'll see how mission is the throbbing heart of Christian friendship, and how we get close to one another not by running after friendship but by marching into battle with each other: spurring one another on, having one another's backs, and binding up each other's wounds.

FELLOW SOLDIERS

In the United States today, the standard military term is four years of active duty, plus four years of reserve service. In the first-century Roman army, the minimum term of service for a legionary rose from sixteen years of active duty to twenty.[2] Soldiering was long-haul work. It was also teamwork. Roman tactics famously depended on formation. Comrades won together, lost together, lived together, died together. The Roman colony at Philippi was established as a place for army veterans to retire and receive the land allotment they had earned. It had deep military roots. It is especially striking, therefore, that Paul writes to the church in Philippi,

> I have thought it necessary to send to you Epaphroditus
> my brother and fellow worker and fellow soldier, and your
> messenger and minister to my need, for he has been longing
> for you all and has been distressed because you heard that he
> was ill. (Phil. 2:25–26)

Paul piles three terms on Epaphroditus: brother, fellow worker, fellow soldier. Like Frodo's threefold epithets for Sam—dear hobbit, dearest hobbit, friend of friends—Paul's description of Epaphroditus builds toward the third descriptor: fellow soldier. We don't know if Epaphroditus had a literal military background. But we do know that he and Paul had fought together side by side in gospel work. As we saw in chapter 3, Paul communicates his love for this comrade when he says that, if Epaphroditus had died, he would have experienced "sorrow upon sorrow" (Phil. 2:27). But his love for Epaphroditus was not possessive: "I am the more eager to send him," Paul writes, "that you may rejoice at seeing him again, and that I may be less anxious" (Phil. 2:28). There is a generosity in Christian comradeship. We must be willing to express our deep attachment to beloved friends while also being willing to support them in the work God puts before them—even if it takes them away from us.

Paul uses fellow soldier language for another friend in his brief letter to Philemon. Archippus was likely Philemon and Apphia's son, but Paul calls him, "Archippus our fellow soldier" (Philem. 2). Paul and Archippus had fought together under Christ. Despite their geographic separation, they're still comrades, and Paul still cares about Archippus' work. At the end of his letter to the Colossians, Paul writes, "say to Archippus, 'See that you fulfill the ministry that you have received in the Lord'" (Col. 4:17).

I'm not pretending this is easy. I've seen dear friends deployed across the world and mourned their absence and how their departure leaves me needing to find other local comrades. Parting is painful. But if we're followers of Jesus, we should not expect an easy life. We're setting our hearts on the day when final victory is declared, and Jesus returns as universal King. Then, we will find our rest in Him and perfect, loving unity with our beloved fellow soldiers. In the meantime, we must go where we're deployed.

The Christian life is a battle, not a retirement plan.

Paul points both to the struggle of soldiering together and the future hope we have in his letters to Timothy. In his first letter, Paul urges his mentee to "wage the good warfare" (1 Tim. 1:18) and to "fight the good fight of the faith" (1 Tim. 6:12). The Christian life is a battle, not a retirement plan. Likewise, in his second letter, he charges Timothy: "Share in suffering as a good soldier for Christ Jesus. No soldier gets entangled in civilian pursuits, since his aim is to please the one who enlisted him" (2 Tim. 2:3–4). But rather than watching from a safe distance as Timothy goes into battle, Paul is calling Timothy to follow in his footsteps. Knowing he will soon be martyred, Paul writes: "I have fought the good fight, I have finished the race, I have kept the faith" (2 Tim. 4:7). Nevertheless, he urges Timothy twice to come and see him soon (2 Tim. 4:9; 4:21).

These snapshots of Paul's relationships with Epaphroditus, Archippus, and Timothy help us understand a vital element of friendship. We are not called to foster friendships solely for their own sake. Rather, Christian friendships are designed to help us fight. Fellow soldiers come alongside each other in the battle. They spur each other on and have each other's backs, and we will need our fellow soldiers in the Lord as we resist an enemy who is far beyond our strength.

Our closest friendships, if we're Christians, should be gospel-spreading partnerships: enduring bonds forged in the fire of shared mission. In a culture that feels starved of friendship, Christians should be living as a counterculture. But our counterculture shouldn't be constructed on a framework of shared leisure time activities, or our enjoyment of the latest Christian songs. Healthy Christian friendships spring up on the battlefield of gospel mission. Conversely, if our friendships with believers consistently draw us back from battle into entertainment mode, they may be quite enjoyable. But they're falling short of Jesus' call.

Don't get me wrong: this doesn't mean that friendship shouldn't offer us an opportunity to rest. In a season of especially intensive work, my dear friend Julie asked, "When do you rest?" I replied, "I'm resting now." I don't drive an electric car. But if I did, I'd need to know the places in my city where my car could get recharged. Likewise, I know the people I can go to when I need to rest: the people who will understand the struggle, because they're in it too; the people who will comfort me and bring me joy. Paul called Epaphroditus both his fellow soldier and "your messenger and minister to my need" (Phil. 2:25). This friend brought Paul both practical help and emotional support. No doubt they rested in each other's company. But rest is not the endpoint for the Christian. It is preparation for the fight. The point of an electric car is not to sit and charge all day. Mission is a joyful fruit of healthy Christian friendship. Conversely, healthy Christian friendship is a by-product of mission.

Does this mean our friends are just a means to an end—like mercenaries paid to make our victory more likely? No. By fighting alongside each other, we enjoy the battle-tested love that soldiers find when they have risked their lives together. This is the kind of friendship love of which there is none greater. It's not sentimental or romantic. It is blood-stained, mud-caked, scratched-up love: the kind for which you'd risk your neck. It's love that picks your brother or your sister up and carries them when they're shot down. It's love that tells them they can stagger on, because they'll have their arm around your shoulder—just like you had your arm around their shoulder the last time you were ready to collapse. When, after months of facing danger side by side, Frodo calls Sam "my dearest hobbit, friend of friends," he's voicing what their friendship has become as they have walked together down a desperate path. If we're honest, we all yearn for this kind of friendship love. But we will only get it if we throw ourselves together into mission, locking step with our comrades in arms. To gain the best friends, we must fight the good fight.

At a low point in the process of writing this book, I texted my friend Sam to say that I was wondering if I should just back out of the contract and declare defeat. It felt too hard and vulnerable, and after two extended deadlines, it still wasn't coming together. Sam texted, "Don't you dare!" and then he gave me the pep talk that I needed. I've played that role for him at times as well. We know that we can call each other when we've lost all confidence in our ability to do the work that God has put in front of us. We can point back to how the Lord has helped us in the past and give each other courage to keep trudging on. Sam is my brother, fellow worker, and fellow soldier. But he's not the only member of my cohort.

FINDING YOUR COMRADES

Rachel and I discovered one another on a cold November evening at Starbucks. We'd met officially at church a year before, but we had never really talked, and nothing in our minor interactions indicated that we needed or much liked each other. Then, a mutual friend told me that we should be friends. So, I initiated coffee. Three things hit me as we talked. First, I found out that Rachel had a stunning testimony. She'd come to faith in Jesus when she was an undergrad at Yale, after her high school girlfriend broke up with her. Rachel's story countered every modern narrative. Unlike the tales of Christians going off to college, embracing same-sex sexuality, and shedding their faith, Rachel had gone to college as an atheist who slept with girls and stumbled upon Jesus. I wanted Rachel's story to be told.

The second thing I noticed was that Rachel was exceptionally smart. Her knack for words is striking. Metaphors bounce out of her like tennis balls from a machine, and she's extremely funny. But it was also evident to me that Rachel loved the Scriptures like few people I had ever met. I felt like a talent scout discovering a fresh, new voice on pressing questions for the church today and wanting that voice to be heard.

The third thing that I realized about Rachel was how much I liked her. We are very different people. Pick any personality test, and Rachel and I come out as basically opposite. I'm an extrovert, she's an introvert. We both love literature, but different kinds. She loves watching sports. I wouldn't care if I never watched a ball fly through the air again. And yet, despite our differences, we get on like a whole apartment block on fire. In meeting Rachel, I felt sure

I'd found a fellow soldier: someone deployed in the same quadrant, with whom I had a natural camaraderie, and who would challenge me as much as I could challenge her.

No doubt, we've all experienced the joy of meeting someone with whom we have great friendship chemistry. You're eager to spend time together and to discover one another's thoughts, ideas, and histories. The question at that point is what to do with all that energy. The answer for a Christian friendship isn't just to turn that energy toward each other—building up your stock of shared experiences and private jokes to hoard your pleasure in each other's company. Instead, the answer is to use that energy as fuel for the work the Lord is calling you to do. Sometimes, you even need that other person to alert you to that calling, and to kick you out into your mission in the world.

I grew up on The Lord of the Rings. In fact, it is one reason why I find faith in Jesus so compelling. The world that Jesus calls me into is an even more adventurous, beautiful, magical world than Tolkien's Middle-earth—and it is real. But were it not for Tolkien's camaraderie with C. S. Lewis, his greatest work would likely never have been published. In a letter to another friend, Tolkien wrote:

> I have never had much confidence in my own work, and even
> now when I am assured (still much to my grateful surprise)
> that it has value for other people, I feel diffident, reluctant
> as it were to expose my world of imagination to possibly
> contemptuous eyes and ears. But for the encouragement of
> C. S. L[ewis], I do not think that I should ever have completed
> or offered for publication *The Lord of the Rings*.[3]

On the one hand, it is wild to think that Tolkien couldn't see how brilliant he was. But at the same time, I can totally relate. Don't worry, I don't have delusions of grandeur that Rachel and I are anything like Tolkien and Lewis! But in our much smaller way, our friendship has pushed both of us to do things we would not have done alone. When we met, she had no sense that she should be writing books and giving talks. She actively avoided public speaking and at first resisted my proposal that she should write up her testimony and subsequently publish a book on Christianity and sexual ethics. It was quite clear to me that God had formed her for this work. But it was far from clear to her.

Conversely, Rachel helps me greatly with my ministry. We share our daily goals. We listen to each other's fresh ideas and moments of discouragement. We read each other's writing and give feedback. With God's help, Rachel flipped from being terrified to speak in front of groups to delivering outstanding talks to large audiences without notes—and her example prompted me to shed the safety blanket of my notes as well. Like soldiers sparring with each other to prepare for battle, Rachel's strengths have helped me grow—and vice versa. I'm always pushing Rachel to write more, instead of hoarding all her knowledge; she's always nagging me to read more.

Frodo called Sam his "friend of friends" because of their shared mission. Likewise, it feels like God has placed me and Rachel shoulder-to-shoulder in the same small corner of His mission in this world. Like an eggshell formed around an embryonic chick, our friendship has been formed around the work that God has given us. It's not that all our Christian friends should be those called to our same field. I gain great encouragement from friends whose calling in this world is different from mine. For instance, my friend Julie stays home with her four daughters and inspires me to love and service in the Lord, while Karolyn works full-time in a demanding secular job and meets with me each week for prayer and mutual accountability. I see the labor in the Lord of friends like these, and it helps me move forward on the battlefield. Their prayers and their example spur me on. But we will all be blessed by friends who understand our kind of work.

Perhaps you're called to foster care and you have one or two companions in the fight who really get the highs and lows of that God-glorifying work. Perhaps you are a scientist, and you've found one or two believers who can understand your academic world and push you to put Jesus first in all you do. Perhaps you're pastoring and you have found a friend who gets how hard that calling is. Perhaps you work in retail, and you have a colleague who is on your mission team as you both seek to serve and witness to your other colleagues and to customers with whom you have the chance to build relationship. Perhaps you're with your kids full-time, and you've found fellow parents who are laboring alongside you—both to raise your own kids in the Lord and to reach those in your networks with the gospel. Or maybe you've retired, and you are busy with the work that God has called you to in this new stage of life.

Last summer, I met a woman who had just entered this stage. She told me she was more pumped to do evangelism than she had ever been before. I thought, "When I retire, I want a friend like her!" We all need fellow soldiers in the quadrant where we've been deployed. But we must all make sure we're fighting the right fight.

FIGHTING THE GOOD FIGHT

The book of Proverbs warns us that the company we keep will shape our character: "Whoever walks with the wise becomes wise, but the companion of fools will suffer harm" (Prov. 13:20). Close friendship can distract us from our mission in this world as thoroughly as it can spur us on. Distraction can look like pursuit of pleasure, wealth, or status, delight in gossip, eroding our defenses against sexual sin, or making politics our greatest passion and our favored politician the focus of our loyalty. Proverbs warns,

> Make no friendship with a man given to anger,
>> nor go with a wrathful man,
> lest you learn his ways
>> and entangle yourself in a snare. (Prov. 22:24–25)

This is true of other kinds of sin as well. But as we look for fellow soldiers, it's especially important that we check we're not aligning ourselves with people who are given to anger and fighting the wrong fight with the wrong weapons.

In his second letter to the Corinthians, Paul gives us a glimpse of the battle in which he is engaged. It is a ministry of reconciliation built on the gospel itself: the truth that "for our sake [God] made [Jesus] to be sin who knew no sin, so that in him we might become the righteousness of God" (2 Cor. 5:21). Paul describes himself facing troubles, hardships, distresses, beatings, imprisonments and riots, hard work, sleepless nights, and hunger (2 Cor. 6:4–5). This is no triumphal victory. It's rough.

So, what's in Paul's armory? He goes on: "By purity, knowledge, patience, kindness, the Holy Spirit, genuine love; by truthful speech, and the power of God; with the weapons of righteousness for the right hand and for the left" (2 Cor. 6:6–7). This passage exposes much of the fighting that Christians do today as antithetical to Scripture. Are we fighting with purity, patience, understanding, and kindness, or are we fighting dirty? Do our friends call us to fight with sincere love and truthful speech, or do they argue that Christianity is under unprecedented attack and that these desperate times require different tactics: grasping at whatever power we can get by any and all means? Is our mission to win our enemies for Christ, or is it to pound them into the dirt? A dangerous false sense of comradeship can arise from gathering allies in the wrong kind of fight. So, how can we spot false comrades from authentic fellow soldiers? Check their armor.

Paul urges the Ephesians to "put on the whole armor of God" (Eph. 6:11). Then, he describes this armor piece by piece. The belt of truth. The breastplate of righteousness. The shoes of the readiness given by the gospel of peace. The shield of faith. The helmet of salvation. The sword of the Spirit, which is the Word of God (Eph. 6:14–17). None of this is brute force. None of it is using the weapons of the world against our enemies. None of it is compromising truth or goodness in pursuit of power. All of it springs from the gospel of peace and the Word of God.

In the same letter in which Paul calls Timothy a "good soldier of Christ Jesus," he writes, "the Lord's servant must not be quarrelsome but kind to everyone, able to teach, patiently enduring evil, correcting his opponents with gentleness" (2 Tim. 2:24–25). These are hallmarks of good Christian leadership. Jesus leads an army stacked with gentle, servant-hearted soldiers, not ruthless hitmen.

We see this gentleness in Jesus when He is arrested. His friends were ready to fight back: "Lord, shall we strike with the sword?" (Luke 22:49). Peter didn't wait for Jesus' response but lashed out and cut off the high priest's servant's ear (Matt. 26:51; Mark 14:47; Luke 22:50; John 18:10). But Jesus said, "No more of this" and touched the man to heal him (Luke 22:51). Jesus wants to raise an army. But not the kind that fights with swords. Instead, He calls us to deny ourselves, take up our cross, and follow Him through suffering and death to resurrection life. But Jesus doesn't call us to face the battle by ourselves. We are sent into the line of fire with our comrades. This partnership is vital to our mission. But sometimes it feels even harder than if we had faced the enemy alone.

> Jesus doesn't call us to face the battle alone. We are sent into the line of fire with our comrades.

FRIENDLY FIRE

There's a moment in The Lord of the Rings when Frodo thinks he needs to carry on without his comrades. A man named Boromir has tried to take the ring, and Frodo can see the power of his enemy at work even among his companions. Sam finds Frodo and insists on going with his master. But even as they journey on together, there are moments when the evil of the ring impacts their friendship. At one point, Frodo accuses Sam of trying to steal the ring when Sam is only trying to help.

Likewise, in the Christian life, the push and pull of comradeship will not be easy. As Proverbs puts it, "Faithful are the wounds of a friend" (Prov. 27:6), and we should expect to be confronted by our fellow soldiers on areas of weakness in our lives. What's more, because we're sinners, we will feel the pain of one another's sinfulness. Paul urges the Ephesians to "be kind to one another, tenderhearted, forgiving one another, as God in Christ forgave you" (Eph. 4:32), and as we'll see in chapter 10, we'll need to exercise the muscles of forgiveness frequently in friendship.

The differences that have made Rachel and me so helpful to each other in a range of ways, combined with each of our besetting sins, have led to many moments when we've misinterpreted, frustrated, or upset each other. The closeness that produces fruitfulness comes with deep vulnerability. As soldiers have each other's backs, they also open themselves up to friendly fire. Just as the evil power of the ring impacted Frodo's comradeship with Sam, our enemy hates Christian friendship and will attack it any way he can. But stumbling upon each other's sin provides an opportunity for growth.

It's common for books on interpersonal relationships to talk about boundaries: the times we must say no to save space for our own needs and not let others trample over us. For years, I struggled with this concept from a Christian point of view. Didn't Jesus call His followers to turn the other cheek if they were slapped across the face on one side? Shouldn't we be ready to give all we have to others, just like He gave all He had to us? Yes and yes. There is a necessary vulnerability bound up in discipleship. We need to love even our enemies and pray for those who persecute us.

But over time, I've realized that if I let my closest Christian friends behave unlovingly to me, I am not loving them. Loving my believing friends means wanting them to grow in godliness. Sometimes, saying no to them will help them recognize their sin, just as the times when they say no to me helps me acknowledge mine. We shouldn't always suck up friendly fire. At times, we need to hold a shield up in between our comrade and ourselves to help them get back into the correct formation. But this correction should be done in love and with their good in mind. It's not about resisting the relationship but advancing it. If we come through the conflict with a clear determination that we'll fight together side by side again, we'll find that we are more effective as a team than we once were.

Partway through their journey to destroy the ring, Sam imagines how their story might be told by a father to his son—if it ends happily: "'Frodo was very brave, wasn't he, Dad?' 'Yes, my boy, the famousest of the hobbits, and that's saying a lot.'" Frodo laughs and points out that Sam has left out one of the main characters: "Samwise the stoutheart." Frodo carries on the dialogue between the father and the son: "Frodo wouldn't have got far without Sam, would he, Dad?" But Sam objects. "'Now, Mr. Frodo,' said Sam, 'you shouldn't make fun. I was serious.' 'So was I,' said Frodo."[4]

chapter five

THE INNER RING

In 1944, C. S. Lewis gave a lecture to students at King's College, London, in which he diagnosed our human tendency to want to get inside exclusive groups. This drive plays out in schools and offices, in churches and on playgrounds, in fraternities and in retirement communities. Membership in the "inner ring" is guarded, so those outside feel their exclusion and are pricked with the desire to enter.

But Lewis notes that when we *do* break into these small worlds, the thrill is fleeting. We may at first swell with the sense that we belong. But soon, we'll start to see another ring inside the ring—an even more exclusive core—and we will find we haven't made the cut. Lewis prescribed an antidote to this poisonous cycle:

> If in your spare time you consort simply with the people you
> like, you will again find that you have come unawares to a

real inside: that you are indeed snug and safe at the centre of something which, seen from without, would look exactly like an Inner Ring. But the difference is that the secrecy is accidental, and its exclusiveness a by-product, and no one was led thither by the lure of the esoteric: for it is only four or five people who like one another meeting to do things that they like. This is friendship.[1]

Lewis's diagnosis is undoubtedly correct: inner rings are real, and their pursuit can be consuming. There is certainly also a place of snugness and security in friendship. But in this chapter, I want to propose a different prescription for those experiencing exclusion from an inner ring. Instead of forming inadvertent inner rings— not aiming for exclusion but achieving it—followers of Jesus find their place of snugness and security by turning toward those who are left out. There is a place for building friendships with people we most naturally like. The energy we gain from those who fill us up can make us able to pour ourselves out in welcome to the lonely and unloved. But if, in our spare time, we only consort with people we like, we won't include the outcasts. Conversely, if we let go of snugness for ourselves, we'll find not only snugness and security, but life and love.

STOP ASKING, "WHO WILL LOVE ME?"

One freezing January evening some years ago, I dragged myself unwillingly to a women's event at our church. I'd recently returned from Christmasing in London to our house in Cambridge, Massachusetts. But it didn't feel like coming home. I'd left extended family and lifelong friends in England. I'd lived in Massachusetts for some years, and I'd accrued some real friends. But most of them had moved away. I felt like I was starved of friendship once again, and I was miserable. I didn't want to go to the event. But I gave myself a pep talk. "Yes, you feel lonely and like you want a closeness you don't have. But ten-to-one, there's someone else who feels that way as well, and you could help her feel more welcomed if you go."

The pep talk turned into a wake-up call: "Stop asking, 'Who will love me?' Instead ask, 'Who can I love?'" I've found this shift to be transformative. When we sit around and think *Who will love me?* loneliness and discontent creep in. But when we give ourselves to loving other people, we will find that love boomerangs back at us when we least expect it.

We find this outside-in approach on the pages of the Scriptures time and again, and it is modeled perfectly in Jesus. As we saw in chapter 2, Paul urged the Roman Christians, "Welcome one another as Christ has welcomed you" (Rom. 15:7). Christ did not wait for us to be desirable before He sought us out. He sought us out when we were nobodies and made us His.

When we welcome people on the outside, we are following in Jesus' footsteps. In His ministry on earth, Jesus didn't focus on the most impressive person in the room. He gave His time to those who'd been rejected and cast out, to the sick and dying, to the poor and the notorious, to any who would only come to Him with all their need. We tend to do the opposite. We find the most important person in the room, according to the standards we most value, and either sidle up to them or sit around and hope that they will notice us.

James exposed this human tendency when he warned Christians against paying more attention to the rich people who show up at church than to the poor (James 2:2–6). We may not think we do this, but we often do. If, like me, you went to university, you might naturally gravitate toward equally educated people at church and inadvertently neglect less educated newcomers. It will take conscious effort not to form an instant inner ring determined by educational or socioeconomic status. This top-down thinking can play out in other ways as well, as we home in on people who have social status based on looks or popularity or age or race or family. But Jesus calls us to a different calculation.

If you want to follow Jesus' priorities, look for the person standing by themselves. The newcomer. The poorer person. Someone who doesn't quite fit with this crowd. The person who is different in age or race or class or first language. The single parent in a sea of married couples. The awkward man who's standing just outside the group. The single woman sitting by herself in church. The parent managing small kids alone while other adults socialize.

Jesus' famous parable of the sheep and the goats reveals that we will meet Him in the people we could help—the poor, sick, or imprisoned (Matt. 25:31–46). In smaller ways, that principle applies in social situations too. Whatever we do for the most neglected person in the room, we do for Him. And when we do, we'll get a taste of the truth of Jesus' enigmatic promise: "Whoever would save his life will lose it, but

> We must reach out in love to welcome others, just as Christ has welcomed us.

whoever loses his life for my sake will find it" (Matt. 16:25).

In his book *The Soul of Shame*, psychiatrist Curt Thompson makes this powerful claim: "We all are born into the world looking for someone looking for us," and "we remain in this mode of searching for the rest of our lives."[2] That searching can be painful. We stand there feeling like we've not been seen. But if we seek the lonely person in the room, we'll find someone who is looking for us, whether they yet realize it or not. We must reach out in love to welcome others, just as Christ has welcomed us. But when we do, we'll find our life both in the people we will meet that way, and in the deeper fellowship we feel with fellow welcomers: the fellow soldiers who are on the lookout for the lonely too. Our goal should not be just to meet one person's need all by ourselves, but to include them in community.

I felt this welcome beautifully myself a few years back. It was my first time speaking at a Gospel Coalition Women's Conference and when I walked into the speakers' room, I saw a group of women sitting around a table. They were all established speakers at the conference and clearly also friends. As I approached the table, I noticed they were wearing matching bracelets. This was a perfect picture of what Lewis pointed to: I'd walked into one inner ring—the speakers' room—only to discover that I was still an outsider. I took a risk and walked up to the table, attempting to make small talk. "What's with the matching bracelets?" Instead of simply answering, Courtney (now my friend) took her bracelet off and gave it to me. It was a tangible expression of her welcome. The inner ring where she belonged was opened up to fit me in. We didn't have a friendship yet. She barely knew me. But she had all the information that she

> We don't just need community with many. We also need connection with a few.

needed: I was on the outside, so she did what Jesus would have done and brought me in.

In one sense, the ring of Christian fellowship must stretch indefinitely. The rock of Jesus' birth, life, death, and resurrection hit our world so hard two thousand years ago that the circle of His followers has been expanding ever since. If we are Jesus' disciples, we should be continually reaching out to welcome others in.

But we don't just need community with many. We also need connection with a few. We thrive in multiple rings of different sizes: perhaps a church of hundreds, a small group of a dozen, and a prayer group of just three. We can propagate the closeness we all need and make space for those on the edges by thinking less in terms of concentric circles and more in terms of chain mail.

CHAIN MAIL

In Lewis's lecture, he describes the disappointment of discovering another inner ring inside that outer one as soon as you break in. As Lewis notes, this is a never-satisfying way to think about relationships. But what if we switch the metaphor from inner rings to chain mail—not the irritating messages that people pressure others to pass on, but the chain mail worn by medieval knights? In these protective garments, every tiny metal circle intersects with other links on every side. The strength of the armor depends on these connections. I can't meet the needs of everyone around me. Nor can you. But together we can ensure that everyone's included.

Last summer, I went to the wedding of two friends in our community group and danced the night away with a bunch of women who are friends with one another and with me. At one point, we joined hands to form a literal ring. But we all also danced in twos and threes. This pictured how we all relate. We meet each Tuesday with our whole community group, which is a mix of men and women including over thirty people and spanning an age range of over thirty years. Everyone is welcome. Those who find it harder to fit in are actively included. But within that larger group, small groups and links develop over time so that each person can feel known and loved.

We try to reinforce a culture of welcome in this group. Each member knows they can invite outsiders to our weekly Bible study and to other purely social gatherings. Newcomers at church, non-Christian friends, roommates, and family members are all welcomed in. We want to be a group with an identity, where members all belong. But part of that identity is that we're always looking to include outsiders. Sometimes, I need to redirect close friends within the group to turn themselves toward those who are struggling to find their place. Sometimes, others in the group have redirected me: drawing me in to love and care for someone I have failed to notice.

When we find ourselves in cozy, Christian inner rings, we must ensure those rings are not ends in themselves, but opportunities to challenge and equip each other for the work the Lord is calling us to do—and that each person in the ring is also reaching out to others to include them in the chain mail.

We all have different levels of capacity and need. You might do well to have one heartfelt conversation with a friend per week, while I thrive best when I have that level of connection almost every day. But all of us will likely thrive if we exist in multiple circles—large and small—and if we reach out to include those on the edges and help them to connect with others too. This isn't always easy.

A few years back, I was involved in planning a women's retreat at our church. I suggested that we share a survey with participants in which we asked them penetrating questions, such as, "Are you struggling with any of the following: depression, anxiety, an eating disorder, alcoholism, drug addiction, suicidal ideation?" One of my fellow planners raised a fair concern: "I don't want us to imply by asking all these questions that we'll be able to meet all these needs if they say yes," she said. In one sense, she was absolutely right. The group of five around that table couldn't meet the needs we might expose by surveying the women of our church. But if the women of the church pooled their resources, we would absolutely have what it would take.

When we stop asking, "Who will love me?" and instead ask, "Who can I love?" it can be easy to get overwhelmed by thinking we ourselves must meet the needs of every person in our reach, and that our needs don't matter. There can even be a kind of pride in thinking that it's our job to care for others, while we're self-sufficient. But that's not how the Christian life is meant to work. Only Jesus can meet everybody's needs. But we together are His body here on earth, and we together have the resources we need to bear each other's burdens (Gal. 6:2).

KNIT TOGETHER

I was sitting in Julie's pristine living room when I asked her for her top three principles on friendship. She paused for a moment. Then she rattled them off: "One, authenticity. I think you need a level of honesty for friendship. Two, availability. You need to make yourself accessible to the other person on a regular basis. Three, I think there needs to be a sense of mission for a Christian friendship to be healthy." A few minutes later, she got up to close a kitchen cabinet door and to straighten her couch pillows (messed up by my son), because she couldn't concentrate with those things in her line of sight. I laughed. It was one reminder among many that Julie and I are very different people. But I think her off-the-cuff principles of friendship are a great place to start.

To cultivate deep friendship, we must spend considerable time with someone. This takes initiation. I have often found that much of the initiation in my friendships falls to me. Texts asking, "Are you free for a playdate this week?" "Do you want to come over for dinner before community group on Tuesday?" or just "How are you feeling today?" Initiation is a vulnerable act. Each time you ask someone to hang out, you risk them saying no. It can be easy if you're mostly taking the initiative to start worrying that no one really wants to spend their time with you—and of course, there will be times when we need to recognize the signs that someone doesn't want to be our close friend. But I've found time and time again that even when I feel like I'm always the one asking, people ultimately say that they've appreciated my initiation. I was once explaining this to someone and I barked across the room to a close friend, "Hey Janine, how did you and I become friends?" She replied, "You kept showing up at my door!"

Likewise, often thanks to my initiation, Julie and I get together often, and with that regularity comes authenticity. We let each other in on what we're doing, where we're struggling, how we're feeling, what we're praying for. But our friendship isn't just an end in itself. It's somewhere we refuel as we support and challenge one another in the mission of our lives. We invest in one another so that we can be, as Paul puts it, "knit together in love."

In Colossians 2:2, Paul uses this powerful metaphor to describe the love that Christians have for one another. Paul tells the Colossians that he struggles for them, for the Christians at Laodicea, and for all who haven't seen him face-to-face, "that their hearts may be encouraged, being knit together in love, to reach all the riches of the full assurance of understanding and the knowledge of God's mystery, which is Christ, in whom are hidden all the treasures of wisdom and knowledge" (Col. 2:2–3).

Paul's purpose in these words is to describe the body of believers in Colossae as a whole, not only individual relationships. But the joining together of the whole body depends on the bonds between individuals as well as on the gathering of the whole church. When we pursue regular, honest, mission-focused friendship, we are creating stitches in the fabric of the church and building up small links in the chain mail that will include each member of the body. And as we do the work of reaching out to build connections across differences of age and taste and life experience, we'll often find ourselves in unexpected friendships, which we would never have discovered if we only focused on the people most like us.

UNEXPECTED FRIENDSHIPS

Two years ago, our pastor let the members of our church know that one woman in our fellowship was dying. Grace and I had worshiped with the same church family for about ten years, but I had never gotten to know her beyond basic pleasantries. When I heard that she'd been diagnosed with terminal cancer, however, I reached out. I wasn't looking for another friend. I knew that Grace was single and about twenty years my senior. Our church trends young, and I was concerned that Grace might lack community as she faced death. So, I invited her over for lunch.

As I talked with Grace that day, I found she'd lived a fascinating life. Born in Malaysia, Grace had lived all over the world. She and her husband, Ravi, had met in Sunday school when they were kids, and they married young. Ravi had died suddenly a decade earlier. As I got to know Grace in the time between her diagnosis and her death, I had the privilege of seeing her approach the ending of her life on earth with calm, inspiring, and unshakable faith. Grace was an aspiring author and she'd written several pieces for a local news outlet, including one about the challenges of telling her young granddaughter that she was going to die. The outlet asked if they could chronicle her death. The last text message I received from Grace read, "They want to do a photo essay and seem keen to follow me to the end. I keep looking and praying for opportunities to speak of my faith."

I know that one day, when I'm facing death myself, I'll think of Grace. I'll think about her faithful witness, even in the last days of her life. I'll think about the joy she took in food and friends and new experiences. I'll think about the times we talked about her suffering and hope and how she longed for resurrection life with Jesus. When I sought Grace out, I had no expectation that we'd build a mutual friendship. I knew she was in need of love, and that I could be one small part of the body of Christ meeting that need. I now know that I'll be forever grateful for the year or so of friendship we enjoyed before she went to be with Jesus. But there will be other times when we reach out to welcome someone on the fringes, and we find them simply difficult to love. That's when we'll need the love of other friends to hold us up.

Last week, I went with my friend Lou and my two younger kids to the climbing gym where Lou's a regular. For hours, he patiently coached and belayed Eliza and Luke. At one point, while Eliza was climbing, I took Luke to the bouldering wall and let him mess around a bit. Without a rope, he could only scramble up a few feet before he had to drop back down to the crash mat. But with Lou belaying him, he could climb twenty or thirty feet, and Eliza could climb over fifty. If we are truly reaching out to build relationships with people unlike us, it will take real effort on our part. If we go solo, we likely won't get far before we come crashing down. But if we have close friends to anchor us, we'll find we can go further and reach farther. Like climbers after an ascent, we'll need to ask our friends to reel us back down periodically for comfort and for rest. But then, we will be ready for another climb.

> If we have close friends to anchor us, we'll find we can go further and reach farther.

You see, when we stop asking, "Who will love me?" we will find that it's not because the answer to that question doesn't matter. It matters greatly. If you are a Christian, you should feel the love of friends who know and love you deeply, as you know and love them. But if each of us moves outward with our love, we'll find that there is more than enough love to go around.

After prescribing spending time with those we like as the antidote to the ongoing quest to penetrate the inner ring, Lewis concluded:

> This is friendship. Aristotle placed it among the virtues. It causes perhaps half of all the happiness in the world, and no Inner Ring can ever have it.[3]

I agree. At least half of my happiness derives from friends. But not because we've made an inner ring to keep the lonely out. Instead (as I have no doubt from his other writings Lewis would agree) it comes from gathering the lonely people into an expansive chain as we all reach out to each other—even when that feels hard—and as we find the welcome with which Christ has welcomed us reflected in the faces of our friends.

chapter six

BODYBUILDING

When I was in college, I rowed. Don't ask me why. I never much enjoyed it, and I lacked the discipline required to get really good. I was naturally strong, and tall enough to do okay, but when my college coach proposed that I do "land training" (weights, etc.), I declined. In fact, the only thing that motivated me to drag my lazy self out of bed at 6:30 a.m. on cold winter mornings was knowing that without me, the rest of my boat couldn't row. Four oars on one side and three on the other simply doesn't work! It's all or nothing.

In one sense, this is a good analogy for Christian fellowship. We need the whole team to show up and pull together, and the boat moves at a speed dictated not by one person, but by everyone. What's more, each person in the boat must synchronize their movements, so their oar enters the water at the same time as their teammates' and they pull at the same rate. The best boats operate like single bodies, with a "cox" sitting in the front of the boat, acting like the head and telling all the rest of the body what to do.

> We need the whole team to show up and pull together, and the boat moves at a speed dictated not by one person, but by everyone.

The Bible gives us this image to help us understand the church: if we are followers of Jesus, we're His body here on earth. In this chapter, we'll look at this repeated metaphor and see how the astonishing claim that Christians are all members of Christ's body impacts Christian friendship. We'll notice how this metaphor helps us recognize our need for one another, what our role in one another's lives should be, and how we should respond when we are envious of someone else's gifts.

BODY IMAGE

In Ephesians 1, Paul draws our eyes to Jesus seated "at [God's] right hand in the heavenly places, far above all rule and authority and power and dominion, and above every name that is named, not only in this age but also in the one to come" (Eph. 1:20–21). But even as our eyes are fixed on Jesus in His cosmic splendor, Paul pulls us up into the image:

> And he put all things under [Jesus'] feet and gave him as head over all things to the church, which is his body, the fullness of him who fills all in all. (Eph. 1:22–23)

If we have put our trust in Jesus, He is our head, and we are His body: bound to Him so fundamentally that nothing in heaven or earth could tear us apart.

In Ephesians 4, Paul uses the body image to explain why Christians should conduct themselves "with all humility and gentleness, with patience, bearing with one another in love, eager to maintain the unity of the Spirit in the bond of peace" (Eph. 4:2–3). "There is one body," Paul argues, "and one Spirit—just as you were called to the one hope that belongs to your call" (v. 4). Our eagerness for unity, which should express itself in humbleness, gentleness, love, and patience toward one another, arises from the fact that we're one body. But unity does not mean sameness. Every body needs a range of different members, and Paul goes on to explain that God gave apostles, prophets, evangelists, shepherds, and teachers "to equip the saints for the work of ministry, for building up the body of Christ, until we attain to the unity of the faith and of the knowledge of the Son of God, to mature manhood, to the measure of the stature of the fullness of Christ" (vv. 12–13).

According to Paul, all Christians in the world today are one body, united by one Spirit. But this is not just a static spiritual reality. It's also a call to bodybuilding. Paul calls the Ephesians to participate in bulking up: "speaking the truth in love, we are to grow up in every way into him who is the head, into Christ, from whom the whole body, joined and held together by every joint with which it is equipped, when each part is working properly, makes the body grow so that it builds itself up in love" (vv. 15–16). So, what does spiritual bodybuilding look like, and what does it have to do with Christian friendship?

BODYBUILDING

Jesus is the ultimate bodybuilder. We only build as workers under Him. But we are called to bodybuilding nonetheless. Participating in the building up of Jesus' body here on earth has two dimensions: evangelism, through which more and more people are brought into the body, and discipleship, which builds the body's strength. Both these kinds of growth can be advanced through Christ-exalting friendships. Both these kinds of growth depend on Christians speaking truth in love: to nonbelievers and to one another. All of this takes discipline.

We have probably all experienced the goodness that results when someone sees our potential and invests in training us up. Whether it's in mathematics, or music, or marathon running, to have someone put effort into learning where we're weak and coaching us to build upon our strengths is a gift. While I did not submit to training like this in rowing, I experienced this gift from one of my undergraduate professors. As I labored on a paper on the mythological figure of Tiresias in T. S. Eliot's *The Waste Land*, this professor gave me several rounds of hard critique. If he had not believed in my potential, he would not have wasted his time on my work. His feedback made the paper better, and I loved him for it. When Paul calls us to speak the truth to one another, he isn't calling us to get a kick out of critiquing others. He's calling us to love each other enough to give corrective feedback.

This kind of love takes knowledge and investment. It may be something we experience in our teenage years or younger adulthood from an older mentor. But many of us as full-fledged adults lack someone older in that mentor role. Instead, we'll find that certain friends step in to push us and correct us and encourage us. To make this possible, we must invite a handful of people into our most tender places: the areas where hurt may hide, and sin may breed. To help us, these friends need to know us well enough to be gentle in the places where we need gentleness and to challenge us in the places where we need correction. Sometimes, this will be in the exact same territory. Often, our strengths and weaknesses are interlaced. It takes detailed knowledge and friend-specific wisdom to distinguish between places where someone needs correction and where they mostly need encouragement. It can take weeks, months, or even years to know another person well enough to recognize the places where these laces have been knotted up and to help them disentangle something true and good and beautiful from the sinful attitudes or habits that have bound themselves around this good.

In my life, for example, I have a great capacity for love and faithfulness to friends. I'll take the good, the bad, the ugly. I'll stick with a friend while they go through depression or anxiety. I'll show up and help out. I'll listen and forgive and try again. But on the flip side of this strength, I have a tendency toward possessiveness and insecurity, both of which can throttle friendship if they're not kept in check. The friends who know me best can help me grow, and they can help me not become discouraged when that growth feels miserably slow.

A few months back, as I was telling Julie how I coach myself when I'm getting sucked into a spiral of negative thoughts, I said, "I hate that I have to go through this process every time. I want to just get to the point where I don't have to do those reps." She said, "Maybe you'll get to that point. But maybe you won't. Perhaps you'll always have to coach yourself like this, and that's okay." Sometimes the progress that our friends can see in us looks like continuing to fight our battles time and time again and not lose heart—whether we are fighting lust or laziness or false beliefs about our own ability to be loved.

I need this kind of feedback in my work as well. I'm naturally impulsive, and I like to improvise more than I like to plan. Mark Zuckerberg's famous motto, "Move fast and break things," suits my style. This means I can be decently productive. It also means I need my closest friends to call me out when I'm just being sloppy. Rachel often helps me by reminding me that I should slow down, work more carefully, and shore up areas of weakness. Because she loves me, she points out where I'm falling short and pushes me to build weak muscles up. We all need people prompting us if we are going to grow.

On Thursday evenings, I meet with my friend Karolyn for prayer, support, and mutual accountability. Karolyn and I are very different people. She's a strong perfectionist and I'm a poster child for done-is-better-than-perfect. There are times when we will slug things out and think the other person is just wrong in their critique. At other times, we'll know they're on the money. We stand up hard to one another. But we will also listen carefully and speak the words of love the other person needs. However strongly we have clashed, we always end our prayer walks with a hug and a spontaneous, "I love you!" Our regular rhythm, our mutual respect, and our deep knowledge of each other's challenges and struggles over several years makes this relationship a blessing to us both.

Our culture says that loving someone means affirming all their choices. Christian friendship at its best can tell a different story: part of loving someone is the willingness to tell them when they're wrong. If I find myself one day on the brink of some disastrous sin, I know that Karolyn will have tracked my steps up to that point, and she'll be standing on the bridge into that sin like Gandalf at the iconic moment in The Lord of the Rings when he shouts out, "You shall not pass!" But to be able to do this, she needs regular, intimate access to my life. We need to arm our fellow soldiers in advance, so they can help us walk away from catastrophic sin, and so they can help us cut out the gangrene of besetting sins in our lives that we might not even be able to see.

Bryan calls the car I drive "the trash compactor" because of all the junk that it accumulates. Honestly, I don't see it. But as I drive my friends around, they point it out. Sometimes, they'll even start to grab the litter and dispose of it to help me out. The sinful patterns in our lives are often like this. We may

> Often, it will take a friend confronting us in love and offering to help for us to even recognize the mess.

be so accustomed to them that we just don't notice. Or we may know that they're there, but justify them in our minds, saying, "It's just how I am." Often, it will take a friend confronting us in love and offering to help for us to even recognize the mess. We need to bear with one another patiently. But we must also speak the truth in love to one another, even when that truth is hard to hear.

God has not designed us to bulk up alone. If we're followers of Jesus, we're one body, and we're meant to need each other. Of course, the body metaphor applies beyond our friendships. It must shape how we relate to everyone within the local church. But the friends who know us best will often be best placed to speak the truth in love. Delightfully, in God's great kindness, Christian friendship isn't just a diagnostic tool—it's also therapeutic. I don't just need my friends to tell me when I need to walk away from sin. I also need their arms around me when I've made that turn.

But what about the times when we feel envious or jealous of our fellow Christians—for what they have or who they are? The body metaphor can help us here as well.

ONE BODY, MANY PARTS

My sister, Rose, is a stickler when it comes to the distinction between jealousy and envy. Use one word when you mean the other in her presence and she'll pounce like an athletic lioness. In case you're rusty on the difference, envy is when we look at what another person has—their gifts, possessions, job, appearance, spouse, children, or friendships—and feel resentful because we don't have what they have. We tend to see envy as a minor sin. But Jesus includes it in His illustrative list of evil things that come out of our hearts and defile us (Mark 7:22).

Jealousy, by contrast, is relational. It's when you don't just fixate on how much you want a spouse *like* your friend's spouse, but when you actually want his or her spouse. It's when you don't just envy the closeness your friend has with someone else, but when you resent their relationship because you feel possessive of your friend.

I tend to be more prone to jealousy than envy, but I vividly remember a spike of envy a few years ago, when a woman in my broader friendship group with whom I had a hard relationship was nailing it on stage. As I sat there in the audience, I felt envy rising to my head like vertigo. I knew it was unrighteous. I should be relishing my sister's gifts, which she was using at that moment to build up the church. Instead, I resented her. I noticed this and searched around for Scripture to reorient my heart. Strangely, the verse that came to mind was Jesus' claim that "where your treasure is, there will your heart be also" (Matt. 6:21). Jesus is warning His followers not to store up possessions here on earth. But His wisdom applies just as well to nonmaterial treasure.

I've found this to be helpful when I'm struggling with envy. Rather than trying to magnify the other person's faults because I hate to see their strengths, I try to ask myself, "How can I invest in and encourage this sibling in Christ?" Transferring treasure into their account helps my heart move from envy to rejoicing in that other person's gift. I don't always succeed. But this principle has helped me when I've stumbled into envy. Sometimes, it's as simple as praying for their continued success. Sometimes, it means actively wading in to help them or encourage them. When you're playing for the same team, cheering on your teammates is part of your job.

Paul uses the body image to make this point yet more intensely: "For just as the body is one and has many members, and all the members of the body, though many, are one body, so it is with Christ" (1 Cor. 12:12). Paul explains that different members of Christ's body have different gifts and different roles, but that this doesn't mean that one member is more precious than another. He invites us to imagine the absurdity of the eye saying to the hand, or the head to the feet, "I have no need of you" (v. 21). He uses this image both to neutralize our envy and to excite our sympathy for one another: "If one member suffers, all suffer together," Paul explains, "if one member is honored, all rejoice together" (v. 26). Paul makes a parallel argument in his letter to the Romans: "For as in one body we have many members, and the members do not all have the same function, so we, though many, are one body in Christ, and individually members one of another" (Rom. 12:4–5).

This body metaphor reveals that envying our Christian friends is not only sinful. It's also stupid. We're not just on the same team. We're one body. Athletes need their different body parts to work both individually and in concert with each other. Excellence in one should cause celebration for another. Injury to one should cause lament for all. Sin clouds our thinking and distorts our feelings. But if we're Christians, we can lean into the truth that we are one with one another in the Lord. Meditating on the body metaphor can help us redirect our thoughts and feelings when the sin of envy surfaces. We don't need to feel competitive. In fact, we desperately need not to.

The body metaphor can also help us fight the sin of jealousy. If we are all one body together, we belong to one another. Today, I may resent the bond between two other siblings in the Lord because I feel left out. But one day, we will all live as one spiritual body in the fullest sense, when Jesus returns and claims us as His bride. At moments when I long for intimacy and find myself in jealous insecurity, I try to redirect my thoughts to this reality. Instead of leaning into jealousy, I can lean into longing for the Lord's return, when we will feel the full delight of being united with one another under Him. Friendship closeness at its best can be a foretaste of this precious intimacy. But when we feel its insufficiency, it points us to that future joy. Meanwhile, we can get on with the building work the Lord has given us.

BUILDING UP

Last year, my husband, Bryan, built a house. He didn't do it solo. There were many workmen chiseling away at various things. But Bryan jumped in about a thousand times to do a range of jobs and to correct mistakes. He called in experts and gave feedback. He laid floors, mudded cracks, and installed windows. As we look around our house today, we see his fingerprints all over it. The rest of us are mostly beneficiaries. But every member of our family made some small contribution, and when the time came for us to move in, our whole community group showed up to move things, and to set up the new home where our group would meet.

According to the Scriptures, Christians are both construction workers and materials for the most stunning building project ever. Like living stones, we're being built up as a spiritual house (1 Peter 2:5). But we're also in the building business. Paul calls believers to build one another up. He urges the Ephesians, "Let no corrupting talk come out of your mouths, but only such as is good for building up, as fits the occasion, that it may give grace to those who hear" (Eph. 4:29). To the Romans, he writes, "So then let us pursue what makes for peace and for mutual upbuilding" (Rom. 14:19), and

"Let each of us please his neighbor for his good, to build him up" (Rom. 15:2). In conversation and in corporate worship, in what we choose to eat and how we share, we need to see ourselves as construction workers tasked with building one another up.

Our goal with close Christian friends must be for them to be built up in Christ. We need not only to be ready to identify their areas of sin and help them cut that gangrene out. We also need to see their strengths and help them grow in their effectiveness. As we think through our friendships, we must ask ourselves: Is being friends with me encouraging this sister or this brother in evangelism?

> **Our goal with close Christian friends must be for them to be built up in Christ.**

Am I exhorting them to be more prayerful and a more devoted student of the Scriptures?

Am I prompting them to be a better friend to others?

If they're married, am I urging them to be a better spouse? If they're single, am I helping them to feel the love of family as they pursue their work under the Lord?

If they have kids, am I resourcing them to be a better parent?

If they have aging parents, am I helping them to be a caring son or daughter?

Am I someone who draws my friends toward materialism, or am I someone who inspires them to be more generous in giving?

We need to ask these questions in reverse as well. If we have Christian friends whose impact on us is that we are less prayerful, less contented in the Lord, less loving toward others, less generous with our money, less concerned to share the gospel with non-Christian friends, we will need to think about how we can reorient those friendships so those answers change. Perhaps we're in a rut of gossiping with certain friends, and we need to bring it up and to confess our sin and set a new trajectory. Perhaps we're married and we're in the habit of complaining in a disrespectful and unloving way about our spouse with certain friends. Perhaps we're single and our time with certain friends stokes discontentment in our singleness. We may just need to voice these things and ask our friend to work with us to change direction. We may, however, need to step back from a friendship if we feel it's mostly causing us to stumble into sin and that the other person isn't open to redirection.

We should not be quick to step back. We must show patience and faithfulness in friendship. But we must also recognize the power of friendship to entice us into sin, and continuing in friendship when the other person is resistant to a redirect is not good for either party. Stepping away from active friendship in these situations doesn't mean denying that this person is our brother or our sister in the Lord or ceasing to want what's best for them. Rather, it means acknowledging that being friends with us is not what's best for them as they continue in discipleship.

Our best friends are directing us to Jesus, not away from Him. They're with us in the trenches when growth looks like fighting the same battles time and time again. They're not looking down on us. They're looking forward with us to the time when we'll be joined with Jesus and with each other perfectly in the one-body unity of resurrection life. When my boat was racing, I would sometimes shout out to our coach, "How much longer?" I was pulling as hard as I could, and I needed to know when it would all be over. As followers of Jesus, we don't know how long our race will be. But we do know that we are in it together—not just as one team, but as one body, united in Christ. While we await His return, let's build each other up in love, because—at the end of the day—we're one body together.

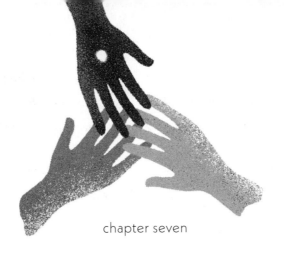

chapter seven

YOUR
UNEXPLORED
SELF

"Will a happy marriage prevent an affair?" In 2017, author and pastor Russell Moore posed this question. Inspired by an *Atlantic* article by influential therapist Esther Perel and his own experience of counseling thousands of couples in crisis, Moore observed that husbands and wives don't cheat primarily because they've had the chance to sleep with someone more attractive than their spouse. Instead, they cheat because the other man or woman offers them an invitation to connect with someone they once were—or could have been. Moore explains:

The secret lover seems to make the married person feel young or "alive" again, until everything comes crashing down. The person is usually not looking for a sexual experience but for an alternative universe, one in which he or she made different choices.[1]

Perel uses the language of the *unexplored self*.[2] "Often," Perel observes, "people cheating on their partners are not sick of their partners—they're sick of themselves."[3]

In this chapter, I want to argue that the inbuilt differences between marriage and friendship are vital to the health of both relationships. Much pain in our society has come from muddling up friendship and marriage: on the one hand, treating sexual relationships as opportunities for exploration with multiple people and on the other hand, devaluing the role of friendship as a place for emotional intimacy and fulfilling exploration. Just as marriage can be ruined by a failure of exclusivity, so friendship can be ruined by a total focus on one friend. But whether we are single or married, friendship can open up new vistas in ourselves as our relationships with friends expand and challenge us and give us a tiny foretaste of the kind of love we'll fully realize one day when Jesus returns.

NONEXCLUSIVE LOVE

In the last chapter, we explored the metaphor of Christians as one body: united to Christ and therefore with each other. This is an expansive vision of connection that sits alongside the other way in which one-body language is used when it comes to human relationships. In his letter to the Ephesians, Paul picks up the metaphor of marriage as a man and a woman becoming "one flesh" in marriage, which is first introduced in Genesis 2:24 and which Jesus quotes when He teaches the spiritual nature of the marriage bond (Matt. 19:6; Mark 10:8). In Ephesians 5:22–32, Paul presses into the metaphor of marriage as a picture of the church as Jesus' body: the exclusive bond between a husband and a wife pictures our union with Christ. In his letter to the Galatians, Paul proclaims that this union with Christ makes many into one with each other, regardless of biological, cultural, or socioeconomic differences: "There is neither Jew nor Greek, there is neither slave nor free, there is no male and female, for you are all one in Christ Jesus" (Gal. 3:28). If we are followers of Jesus, we are called into expansive love.

Paul models this when he declares to the Philippians, "God is my witness, how I yearn for all of you with the affection of Christ Jesus" (Phil. 1:8). Later, he calls them "my brothers, whom I love and long for, my joy and crown . . . my beloved" (Phil. 4:1). Paul voices his effusive love to a whole church. But in the same epistle, Paul highlights individual relationships in which he has invested: for instance, with Timothy and with Epaphroditus. As we have seen in this book so far, the Bible calls us to a depth of love in Christian friendship that we seldom reach. But because of our human limitations this side of eternity, we'll never plumb these depths if we attempt to spread ourselves equally between all possible friends. At the same time, it's important that we don't make the mistake of piling all the deep affection that the Bible calls us to on just one brother or sister. Like a magnifying glass that focuses the sunlight on one spot and starts a fire, we will ultimately damage our relationships if we do. Unlike marriage, friendship by its nature is various and free.

I don't mean to imply that friendship is disposable—like paper cups compared to the champagne glasses of more permanent relationships. As we've seen already in this book, the bonds of friendship can be both durable and life-giving, and while marriage should be lifelong, it won't last into eternity. But while there is security and joy in my belief that my husband, Bryan, won't abandon me regardless—and while a healthy marriage requires that a husband and a wife choose one another in a meaningful, ongoing sense—there's a different kind of joy in knowing my close friends are freely choosing to invest in me, when they could make another choice.

My personality is such that I can twist this joy. There have been times when I have felt like every time I see a friend, I needed to be maximally funny, smart, supportive, kind, and interesting if I'm going to make the grade. My friends have sometimes had to reassure me that this isn't true. They love me even on my least compelling days, and there's good evidence from studies in psychology that being vulnerable actually makes us more likeable, so sometimes letting friends in when we feel least lovable actually increases their love.[4]

But at the same time, friendship often brings out the best in us precisely because we know our friends are freely choosing us. "People are at their most generous, their funniest, and their most fascinating when talking with and about their friends," wrote journalist Julie Beck in a series of interviews for *The Atlantic* called "The Friendship Files."[5] We rise to the occasion of our friends in ways that cultivate our best selves—if we're steering one another toward goodness and not sin. And while there's risk inherent in the fact that a person you feel close to hasn't made a lifelong promise to be there for you, for better or for worse, there's also pleasure in the knowledge that your friends are freely choosing to be close to you. If you're anything like me, you'll sometimes struggle with that tension. One night, when my son Luke was just a few months old and I was still in the throes of nighttime feedings, I checked my phone and saw a screen-long text from Julie. This was atypical. Julie and I mostly text to schedule playdates and we'd had one earlier that day in which I'd shared some vulnerable things. When I saw Julie's text, my instant thought was that she was telling me she needed to step back from our friendship. In fact, her text was nothing of the sort. It was a praise report on answered prayer. I realized in that moment quite how deeply I believed my closest friends are just one step away from ditching me. "I think I assume our friendship is hanging by a thread," I explained when I next saw Julie, while laughing at my knee-jerk dash to insecurity. "It's not hanging by a thread," she replied. "It's hanging by a rope. Made of steel."

In my defense, this fear is grounded in experience. I've been through friendship break-ups that have felt at the time just like a straw that broke an unknown camel's back, or when a close friend simply ghosted me. I've learned with time that some-

> Deep friendship takes great risk. The more we trust and give our heart, the more we risk it being broken.

times it's the other person's issues that precipitate the break. I've walked with certain friends through seasons of profound depression or anxiety. In some cases, it has made our friendship closer.

In others, they have cut me out, along with other people who were close to them. Deep friendship takes great risk. The more we trust and give our heart, the more we risk it being broken. But despite this, it's worth forging onward into friendship, and we can learn to mitigate the risk in healthy ways.

PIZZA

At my lowest point last summer, I sent an SOS to an old friend in England. Laura was three years ahead of me at Cambridge and she read the Bible with me weekly in my first year as an undergrad. My eighteen-year-old self was in awe of her. Since then, we've formed a reciprocal friendship. Several years ago, she asked if I'd be up for a prayer partnership. She needed a trusted Christian friend outside of her day-to-day. I said, "Yes, please! So long as it was a no-holds-barred arrangement, where we each commit to sharing our most shameful sins and struggles." Laura agreed. We're both extremely busy people with three kids, demanding jobs, and different time zones, so we don't have fixed connection times. Instead, we operate like mutual emergency services.

On this occasion, I rapid-fired my thoughts and fears and craziness to Laura, while I paced around my neighborhood. I told her how frustrated I was that I'd had a resurgence of old friendship insecurities two weeks before beginning work on a friendship book. She gave me all the reassurance and encouragement I needed in the moment. Then, I tested out a metaphor I'd dreamed up for this book. "Imagine a pizza," I said. "The slices can be different sizes, but each slice cuts right to the center. I think that's a helpful metaphor for friendship. Some friends will have more of your time and energy than others. You may even have one friend who regularly has the largest slice. But if you do, it's vital that you have other friends who also get to cut right to the center of your heart, or else you end up with an exclusivity that tends toward unhealthiness." I'd been toying with this metaphor for months, and I was pleased with it. Laura replied, "I think it's a terrible metaphor. It pictures friendship as a zero-sum game. Forget your pizza!"

Laura's pushback has some legs. The downside of the pizza metaphor is that a larger slice to one friend means a smaller portion of the whole remains for others. There's some degree of necessary truth to this. As finite beings, any hour we spend with one friend is an hour we didn't spend with others. But as Laura pointed out, we shouldn't picture Christian friendship as competitive. Rather, our friend's other friends should be an asset to our friendship.

The day after Laura trashed my pizza metaphor, I tried it on two other friends. Paige and Julia have very different personalities. Paige, like me, is prone to friendship insecurity. Julia, like Laura, isn't. Paige and I begin with the assumption that our friends might ditch us any day. That thought does not occur to Julia. She knows that she's a great friend and she also knows she needs her freedom. Julia and Paige are close friends, and we laughed about our differences. But they both liked the pizza metaphor.

You see, we all thrive best when we grant multiple friends access to our deepest thoughts and feelings—even if one friend might cut into that core more frequently than others or occupy a larger slice of our time. I tend toward exclusivity. I work hard to make sure people on the fringes feel included, but at the same time,

I'm prone to thinking that I need one closest friend who hangs out in my core and gives me an exclusive season pass to theirs. Sure, other people get to crunch the crust, but I alone get access to my friend's most tightly guarded inner self. Conversely, I will worry that a friend with whom I've shared *my* inner self might find she doesn't want me anymore and exercise her freedom to find someone else with whom to share her heart. Its seed is insecurity, and its fruit can be unhealthy codependency: an ultimately stifling relationship where people find they lose their own identity because of their extreme attachment to the other person. I've been there and done that. I've also walked with friends who've found themselves in that situation.

RESISTING CODEPENDENCY

I was once counseling a friend who was years into an unhealthy codependency. I said of her other friend, "I think she needs to work out who she is when you're not there." My friend replied, "I don't think I know who I am when *she's* not there." That feeling is the crux of codependency. It can arise in various relationships: parent-child, romantic relationships, or friendships. It can disguise itself as healthy intimacy. But it gradually shrinks both parties down to where they only operate as one. This is destructive in romantic partnerships and crippling in friendship. But it can be hard to differentiate the path to closeness from the path to codependency. The key to navigating here is how we each relate to other people. Are we harnessing that friendship love and using it to turn us and our close friend out to love the people in our path, or are we turning all that closeness inward, to reinforce our bond? If our best friend is unavailable, will we take present needs to someone else, or will we linger in the dark until that one friend meets our needs again?

I've ruined friendships with wrong answers to these questions. What I've learned is that it's vital to invest in multiple close friends. I remember one occasion when I felt like I was walking through molasses to turn myself toward another friend, when I was sensing a desire for codependency with one friend starting to suck me in. Friendship can lean toward idolatry when we seek one friend to meet all our emotional needs.

> Are we harnessing that friendship love and using it to turn us and our close friend out to love the people in our path, or are we turning all that closeness inward, to reinforce our bond?

This warning against codependency is not a warning against closeness. As we've already seen, the Scriptures are quite clear that closeness between Christians is a vital good. It's also not a warning against spending extra time and energy on certain friends. We don't possess an inexhaustible reserve for friendship. We're bound by time and mental and emotional space. We need to nurture other kinds of bonds, whether with spouses, parents, children, or colleagues. But for those of us who can feel the pull of codependency, it's helpful to remember that those other friendships need not take away from our relationship. In fact, they can enhance it.

My friend Rachel reads voraciously. This makes her fascinating company. She brings ideas to me that she has gleaned from books. But she also brings ideas from conversations she has had with other people. When I relate to Rachel, I am gaining from her other friends. To stretch the pizza metaphor a bit, the total pizza of my friend expands from all her other interactions, so the slice I get is bigger than it would have been, not smaller from her time with other people. Likewise, I become more interesting when I engage with people and ideas instead of sitting in my room reflecting on how boring and inadequate I am! At the end of the day, while our eternal value is completely set by Jesus' eternal love for us, we're all quite boring in and of ourselves. But when we interest ourselves in other people, we not only help them feel more cared for—we also grow in our ability to bring fresh insights and ideas to those around us.

Perhaps, instead of pizza, we should think of friendship more like hunter-gathering. We go out in the world each day and pick up new experiences. We talk and read and think and watch and feel and then we come back to our friends and say, "Hey, look at this cool thing I found!" or "Here's a cut I got from when I tried to hunt that wildebeest. It really hurts." When I can set aside the piece of me that lurches into insecurity, my friendships thrive, and friends come back to me with what they've found. I tried this second metaphor on Paige and Julia. "I always worry that they won't come back," Paige answered. I replied, "Me too!" That is the risk in friendship. But when friends do return, I feel the pleasure of their company the more for knowing that they didn't do it out of duty, but from choice. The beauty of marriage is that it's locked in and exclusive. The beauty of friendship is that it isn't. Marriage and friendship are designed to complement, not replicate each other. Their basic protocols are different. But our closest friendships can be just as close as spousal relationships. Conversely, healthy friendships can save marriages.

YOUR UNEXPLORED SELF

When Julie was delivering her fourth child, I babysat her other kids. To thank me, Julie gave me a brightly colored, mostly orange, flowery coffee mug. "It made me think of you," she said. I asked her why on earth that was. I mostly wear dark colors, and I didn't have a single flowery item to my name! Julie replied, "I know. But I can tell there are all these colors inside you, just waiting to come out!" So far, she's wrong. I still wear darks and don't own any flowery things except her coffee mug. But I drink from it every morning and enjoy this tiny invitation to explore an unexplored dimension of myself. This is a trivial example. But our friends can open up such vistas frequently.

My closest friends who know my inner life are also drawing me to be a better version of myself. My newest or most geographically distant friends can likewise play a part, as I connect with different people's hearts and minds. The promise of adventure, the desire to be newly known and loved, and the freshness of variety need not be packaged in the death trap of affairs. Instead, it can be brought to us in friendship as we see and know and love the range of people God has brought into our lives. Friends can be those with whom—in healthy ways—we *do* explore our unexplored self.

No single human is equipped to draw us out in all the good ways we could be drawn. If you are married now, your husband

> Friends can be those with whom—in healthy ways—we *do* explore our unexplored self.

or your wife is not designed to be your all-in-all—or to enable you to be all you could be. While spouses are required to be each other's world in sexual terms, they're not supposed to be each other's world relationally. If you are single, don't be fooled by that imaginary vision of what spousal love should be. If you're married, don't be disappointed that your husband or your wife is not as endlessly fascinating as you might once have thought they were. They need more than you and you need more than them, and you'll both gain when each of you has room to grow. Affairs for married people or illicit sexual relationships for singles can draw us out in sinful ways into an alternative, nostalgic, or transgressive version of ourselves. But friends can draw us in delightful, healthy ways to be the person we could be.

To make an analogous point, psychologist Marissa Franco quotes French Cuban author Anais Nin, who writes, "Each friend represents a world in us, a world possibly not born until they arrive, and it is only by this meeting that a new world is born." Franco goes on to explain "self-expansion theory"—which suggests that "our identity needs to be constantly expanded for us to be fulfilled, and relationships are our primary means for expansion."[6] But as with so many other discoveries of modern psychology, when we look back to the Bible, we find that it has all the ingredients for human flourishing laid out for us.

When we live into the biblical call to love within the body of Christ by making new friends and building up existing friendships, we have opportunities to grow and stretch ourselves in fresh and God-exalting ways. Conversely, when we look to marriage as the only real locus of connection, we find ourselves impoverished. Franco comments from her own experience: "Even in my greatest romantic relationships, when I haven't seen friends enough, I've felt my personality accordion inward. One person, no matter how great, could surface only one side of me. Hanging out with different friends dilated my personality like a peacock fanning its tail."[7]

Multiple studies in psychology have found that people "are more resilient to negative events within their romantic relationships when they have friends."[8] Married or single, we humans all need love from multiple directions, and if we find true love in God-glorifying friendships we will be less liable to fall for the false love on offer in sexual relationships outside of marriage. We'll dig more into how this echoes what the Scriptures teach in chapter 8. But ultimately, only God will satisfy our deepest longings for variety and freshness and exhilarating love.

> When we live into the biblical call to love within the body of Christ by making new friends and building up existing friendships, we have opportunities to grow and stretch ourselves in fresh and God-exalting ways.

Almost two thousand years ago, Jesus declared:

"Truly, truly, I say to you, an hour is coming, and is now here, when the dead will hear the voice of the Son of God, and those who hear will live. For as the Father has life in himself, so he has granted the Son also to have life in himself." (John 5:25–26)

Jesus is the only human who has "life in himself." All other people— even those we're most drawn to—are only living as an overflow of Jesus' intrinsic life. But as we lean into the love of Jesus and move forward in His mission in this world, we'll find His love refracted in the love of those around us. The followers of Jesus are His body here on earth, deriving life from Him and sharing in His love. As we get close to one another, we experience—in an imperfect way— the love that Jesus has for us.

When I called my friend Laura in to help in my distress, I was also reconnecting with a younger version of myself. She was the Christian whom I most admired when I was eighteen. She was studying the same subject as me and well known for her brilliance and popularity, as well as for her faith. Six feet tall, she towered over me in stature and in status as a senior in college. I grew in many ways through knowing her. Now I'm a friend whom she can turn to for support when things are hard, just like I can turn to her. She knows my deepest fears and darkest thoughts. But she can call me to my better self, because—in God's great kindness—she is part of making it.

chapter eight

BROTHERS AND SISTERS

"I have a gift certificate to a nice steakhouse. Let's eat there!"

I had a speaking engagement in Nashville, so I'd texted my friend Sam to see if he was free to get together. Sam and I have been good friends for several years. I'm married. Sam is single. We're both Brits and within a few years of each other's age. No doubt, the restaurant staff at the fancy steakhouse in Nashville thought we were a couple. But in addition to the fact that I am married, Sam and I are both same-sex attracted, so the chances of us forming a romantic bond are pretty close to zero. I can hang out with Sam just like I'd hang out with my biological brother. We can confide in one another freely and express our mutual fondness without fear of misinterpretation. But the utterly straightforward friendship I experience with Sam can't be assumed in many friendships between men and women.

Even if there isn't a risk of mutual attraction, attraction on one side can make what feels like friendship to one party feel more like a space for cultivating sexual desire to the other. Those of us who are primarily attracted to folks of our same sex may find male-female friendship easier. But by the same token, certain same-sex friendships can become sites of sexual temptation.

So, how are we to navigate this fraught terrain? Should meaningful male-and-female friendship just be out of bounds—like the Forbidden Forest in the Harry Potter series? Should those of us with the capacity to be attracted to same-sex friends pull back from all such friendship as a safeguard? I don't think so.

In this chapter, we'll explore the challenges and opportunities of friendship between men and women, and for Christians who experience same-sex attraction. We'll recognize the pitfalls on both sides of the terrain and see how Scripture helps us both to flee from sexual sin and to form God-glorifying friendships with our brothers and our sisters in the Lord.

THE PAUL RULES

In 1948, the evangelist Billy Graham and three of his ministry companions agreed on four rules that would protect their ministry from being torn apart by sin. The first rule focused on the lure of money; the third on the importance of local church, and the fourth on the corrupting power of fame. But it's the second rule that has gained a life of its own. In his autobiography, Graham explains the second rule like this:

> We all knew of evangelists who had fallen into immorality while separated from their families by travel. We pledged among ourselves to avoid any situation that would have even the appearance of compromise or suspicion. From that day on, I did not travel, meet or eat alone with a woman other than my wife. We determined that the Apostle Paul's mandate to the young pastor Timothy would be ours as well: "Flee . . . youthful lusts" (2 Timothy 1:22, KJV).[1]

This principle of never meeting alone with someone of the opposite sex except your spouse has since been codified as "the Billy Graham rule" and used by many Christians. Graham cites 2 Timothy 1:22 as a theological justification for this rule, but he could have drawn on other New Testament texts. Christians are called to flee from, put to death, and take drastic measures to cut out sexual sin (1 Cor. 6:18; Col. 3:5; Matt. 5:27–30). But these stark warnings are not all the Scriptures have to tell us about male-female relationships outside marriage.

While Paul does tell his mentee Timothy to flee from youthful passions, he doesn't tell him to flee from all relationships with women. Rather, he urges Timothy to encourage "older women as mothers, younger women as sisters, in all purity" (1 Tim. 5:2). Mother-son and brother-sister bonds are not sexual, but they're deeply loving. Paul tells Timothy to cultivate these bonds. Paul modeled this himself. As we saw in chapter 2, he called individual women like Phoebe and Apphia "our sister" (Rom. 16:1; Philem. 2).

What's more, while he calls three men "my beloved" in his letter to the Romans (Rom. 16:5, 8, 9), Paul only slightly modifies the expression when he greets a woman: "Greet the beloved Persis, who has worked hard in the Lord" (Rom. 16:12). It's possible that the difference of "my beloved" versus "the beloved" hints at some degree of differentiation.[2] But Paul's warmth toward Persis and other spiritual sisters is unmistakable.

Rather than seeing women primarily as temptresses, Paul evidently valued them as gospel partners. As we saw in chapter 3, Paul commended his sister-in-the-Lord Phoebe to the Romans as a patron to many, including Paul (Rom. 16:1–2). He goes on to honor multiple other women. He hails a married couple, Prisca and Aquila, as "my fellow workers in Christ Jesus" (v. 3) and he greets "Andronicus and Junia, my kinsmen and my fellow prisoners" commenting that "they are well known to the apostles, and they were in Christ before me" (v. 7). This man and woman had been imprisoned with Paul—a state of deepest comradeship—and he had profound respect for them. Likewise, Paul greets two sisters as "those workers in the Lord, Tryphaena and Tryphosa" (v. 12), and he highlights "Mary who has worked hard for you" (v. 6). Rather than just admiring their gospel work from a distance, Paul seems to have worked very closely with some women.

> Rather than seeing women primarily as temptresses, Paul evidently valued them as gospel partners.

In his letter to the Philippians, Paul addresses two women, Euodia and Syntyche, and urges them to "agree in the Lord" (Phil. 4:2).

Much ink has been spilled on how exactly these women were not agreeing. But rather than casting them as troublemakers, Paul sees them first and foremost as his gospel partners. Paul continues, "Help these women, who have labored side by side with me in the gospel together with Clement and the rest of my fellow workers, whose names are in the book of life" (Phil. 4:2–3).

The word translated "labored side by side" means to strive or labor together with someone. Paul uses the same verb earlier in the letter, when he looks forward to hearing that the Philippians are "standing firm in one spirit, with one mind striving side by side for the faith of the gospel" (Phil. 1:27). A vigorous togetherness in mission has characterized Paul's relationship with Euodia and Synthyche. They are his fellow workers, serving side by side with Paul. Just as mission forms the center of close same-sex Christian friendships, so our mission in the Lord should be the glue between believers of the opposite sex. So, where does this leave us when it comes to Billy Graham's second rule?

BROTHER-SISTER BONDS AND BOUNDARIES

It's popular today to criticize people who follow the Billy Graham rule. For one thing, it can oversexualize male-female conversation. For another, it can perpetuate a boys-club feel in ministry, as male mentors only build relationships with younger men, while women who could benefit from mentorship get frozen out. I get both these critiques and want to give them their due weight. At the same time, it seems to me that Graham was wise: in his specific circumstances, with his calling and his culture, his rule was likely helpful.

If any man or woman thinks the Billy Graham rule is right for them, I support them. I don't know the sexual struggle someone else might face and I have no desire to undermine their fight against sin. Just as an alcoholic must avoid all alcohol, some people may be best to avoid all one-on-one relationships with people they might find attractive. Conversely, I can fully understand a woman who has been sexually assaulted or abused wanting to avoid all situations (like a car ride) where she's one-on-one with a man. This doesn't cut out all male-female friendship. It's quite possible to build up bonds of friendship without spending time alone with someone. But rather than a blunt, one-size-fits-all approach, I think we need to figure out a set of principles that help us run far and fast from sexual sin while robbing none of us of the good things that God might have for us in friendship.

For brothers and sisters of a similar age, our aim should be to build up sibling bonds. For instance, Lee is one of my best friends from seminary. He now lives in Malawi with his wife and son and serves the Lord there. We don't get to see each other often face-to-face, but we will sometimes message or catch up by phone, and when we do, we gladly share more personal things and tell each other that we love each other. We've been friends for long enough and know each other well enough that there's no fear of misinterpretation.

When I relate to married male friends, I always keep an eye out for the health of their marriage and make sure I'm not stepping into an unhealthy place without realizing it. But with this eye wide open, I feel free to build real friendships. Likewise, when I relate to single men at church, they know my friendliness is not flirtation.

For brothers or sisters who are substantially younger than us, we should feel a parent-like care. I get to experience this in our community group, where the youngest adult member is an undergrad. Andrei is young enough to be my son and I relate to him and to the other younger men within our group that way. I don't feel much concern that they will misinterpret me if I show signs of warmth to them. In fact, as single men in our society tend to be particularly starved of physical affection, I gladly hug my younger, son-like brothers in the Lord. Sadly, were our sexes reversed, I'd need to be more careful.

In 2017, *The Economist* ran an article titled "What's the Best Age Gap in a Relationship?," which cited a study conducted by the dating website OkCupid. The study found that "while female users look for men roughly the same age as them (or perhaps a year or two older) men prefer women in their early twenties, regardless of their own age."[3] It's hardly breaking news. We see the evidence of older men's desire for younger women throughout history and across cultures, and sadly—for all our talk of equality between the sexes—twenty-first-century Western culture has not achieved equality in this respect. As we relate to brothers or sisters substantially older or younger than us, we need to take account not only of how we might feel toward them, but also of how they might feel toward us.

I recently met for coffee at an airport with a pastor friend eight years my senior. Our only previous in-person meeting was when social distancing was strongly recommended. He asked, "Are you a hugger?" in a way that gave me the option to say, "No." I appreciated this. I felt fine to hug him, but there might well be other situations where I would say no to physical affection from an older man.

We will love each other best if we think first about the other person's comfort. Paul's command to the Philippians—"Let each of you look not only to his own interests, but also to the interests of others" (Phil. 2:4)—should be our guide. It's in our interests to flee any hint of sexual immorality, so we should check our own hearts. But we also need to maximize the interests of others. This will mean not crossing boundaries that might either trigger them sexually or make them feel uncomfortable because they aren't quite sure what's happening on our side. Ultimately, we are each responsible for ourselves and not the other person. Women have sometimes been made to feel like they are responsible for men's sexual feelings toward them. We are not. But whether we are male or female, we must all do our best to be sensitive to other people's vulnerabilities.

The question we must always ask is, "What does love look like in this situation?" The sex of the two parties will certainly play into this, but it won't always spit out the answer. There have been moments when I've sensed I needed to be careful with some female friends because of their same-sex attraction or my own. But while we must flee from sexual immorality, we must be careful not to run away from gospel-centered friendship based on fear. If we let fear set the agenda, we can end up oversexualizing all male-female interactions because we don't have healthy models in our lives of what true brother-sister friendship looks like.

So, what about same-sex friendships for Christians who experience same-sex attraction?

SAME-SEX RELATIONSHIPS

"Why don't you just choose not to be friends with women you're attracted to?" This question came from a dear friend of mine from college days. When I was at university, I kept my experience of same-sex attraction almost completely to myself. So, Kate (one of my closest Christian friends in college) was on my list of people I should tell when I eventually decided this was not the best approach. Her question was reasonable. You'd think it would be easy for a Christian who, like me, is drawn romantically to others of their same sex to just nip that in the bud. Meet a woman you find attractive: strike her off your friendship list. Meet a woman you're not attracted to, and bingo: there's a possible, uncomplicated friend! But it's not that simple. I can think of many times when I've met a woman who has struck me from the first as beautiful and grown a friendship that is totally straightforward. At other times, I've met a woman and thought she wasn't someone I would ever be attracted to, but later found I was. It's not just me. I recently met a single brother, who shared precisely that experience: the unpredictability of attraction cropping up in same-sex friendship. So, what are same-sex attracted believers like him and like me to do?

One answer is to avoid all same-sex friendship. I've heard from multiple same-sex attracted Christians over the years who have withdrawn from all real closeness out of fear. But I don't think this is the answer. I believe that close, same-sex friendships are a precious gift from God available to all believers, and we're letting Satan rob us of that gift if we withdraw from meaningful connection. For same-sex attracted Christians, claiming this gift can be more complicated.

It requires knowing yourself well and being known by others, who will show up for you when you need help to stay on friendship's path and not stray off into sexual desire. But this is true for heterosexual Christians too. We all need help from our comrades in arms.

I've shared already that I meet weekly with my dear friend Karolyn to walk and pray. I make sure she knows any time I find myself even remotely attracted to someone in my orbit. Even if there isn't any present threat, I want to flag the future possibility so she will know to ask hard questions down the road. Affairs are seldom sudden leaps. They're usually a sequence of small steps, and I want Karolyn to know if there is someone in my friend group who might theoretically take me down that path. I'd recommend that level of accountability to you if you're attracted to the opposite sex as well. Our friends can truly help us guard our hearts and minds from sexual sin. Of course, we can ignore their wisdom. When Rachel, early in her Christian life, had planned a trip to visit her ex-girlfriend in New York, an older Christian friend asked her, "What will you do if she tries to kiss you?" Rachel was taken aback. She thought she was secure in her commitment to the Lord and no longer vulnerable to this past relationship. But she found out the answer to her friend's penetrating question that weekend, when she discovered quite how unprepared she was to face that situation. I've sometimes asked myself this question too. You see, to guard ourselves from sexual sin, we don't just need to guarantee that we won't take initiative to turn a friendship sexual. We also need to ask ourselves what we would do if that initiative was taken by the other person.

It might be tempting to conclude that it would just be better to avoid close friendship generally, for fear of messing up. But when we starve ourselves of friendship, we are left *more* vulnerable to sin. Sexual sin is often fed by loneliness. When I experience affectionate relationships with multiple close female friends, I'm actually shoring up my defenses. I know that I am loved and wanted by my sisters in God-glorifying ways, so I'm not hungering to fill that void in sinful ways.

Reflecting on her early experiences of Christian community, Rachel wrote this about her college friends: "One of the most helpful things was all the physical affection displayed in the group. My friends overflowed with hugs! And it was common for women in the group, when hanging out, to show casual physical affection as a form of love. It happened more than once that I fell asleep with my head on a friend's lap."[4] As a follower of Jesus, Rachel had walked away from sexual relationships with other women. But the outcome was more love, not less, as she found deep connection and affection with her sisters in the Lord. Whatever form our sexual temptations take, if we search the Scriptures, we will find the antidote to sexual sin is not relational starvation. It is love.

> When we starve ourselves of friendship, we are left *more* vulnerable to sin.

A CALL TO BROTHERLY AND SISTERLY LOVE

The modern mantra "Love is love" is contradicted by the Scriptures not only because they rule out all sexual activity outside male-female marriage (e.g., Mark 7:21; Rom. 1:24–32; 1 Cor. 6:9; 1 Tim. 1:10), but also because they strongly urge us to pursue a different kind of love. The prohibitions and commands are often in proximity. For instance, in his first letter to the Thessalonians, Paul writes:

> For this is the will of God, your sanctification: that you abstain from sexual immorality; that each of you know how to control his own body in holiness and honor, not in the passion of lust like the Gentiles who do not know God; that no one transgress and wrong his brother in this matter, because the Lord is an avenger in all these things. (1 Thess. 4:3–6)

Immediately after issuing this stark warning against sexual sin, Paul writes,

> Now concerning brotherly love you have no need for anyone to write to you, for you yourselves have been taught by God to love one another, for that indeed is what you are doing to all the brothers throughout Macedonia. But we urge you, brothers, to do this more and more. (vv. 9–10)

In almost the same breath as Paul warns Christians about sexual immorality, he calls them deeper into brotherly love (*philadelphia*).

It's no exaggeration to call 1 Thessalonians a love letter. Paul writes, "Being affectionately desirous of you, we were ready to share with you not only the gospel of God but also our own selves, because you had become very dear to us" (1 Thess. 2:8). He speaks of his pain at their separation: "Since we were torn away from you, brothers, for a short time, in person not in heart, we endeavored the more eagerly and with great desire to see you face to face, because we wanted to come to you" (vv. 17–18). What's more, Paul prays for them to "increase and abound in love for one another and for all, as we do for you" (1 Thess. 3:12). One of the primary relationships in which we will give and receive this brotherly love is in our same-sex friendships. Whatever our patterns of attraction, the community into which Jesus invites us has more love than the world can offer us—not less.

Time and again in the New Testament, we see both the call to love between believers and the warning against sexual immorality. In Ephesians 5, Paul calls his readers to be imitators of God, and to "walk in love, as Christ loved us and gave himself up for us, a fragrant offering and sacrifice to God" (Eph. 5:2). He then immediately contrasts this love with sexual immorality: "But sexual immorality and all impurity or covetousness must not even be named among you, as is proper among saints" (v. 3). Paul goes on to offer another contrast of behaviors: "Let there be no filthiness nor foolish talk nor crude joking, which are out of place, but instead let there be thanksgiving" (v. 4). Just as thanksgiving is the antidote to filthiness and crude joking, so love is the antidote to sexual immorality.

We see a similar contrasting of ideas in Galatians 5, where Paul writes, "Now the works of the flesh are evident: sexual immorality, impurity, sensuality, idolatry, sorcery, enmity, strife, jealousy, fits of anger, rivalries, dissensions, divisions, envy, drunkenness, orgies, and things like these" (Gal. 5:19–21a) then immediately contrasts this list of sins with the fruit of the Spirit: "love, joy, peace, patience, kindness, goodness, faithfulness, gentleness, self-control" (v. 22–23a). Sexual immorality began the list of works of the flesh, and love heads up the list describing the fruit of the Spirit.

If Sam and I were following the Billy Graham rule, we wouldn't have the healthy, brother-sister friendship we enjoy, and we'd be missing out. But our opposite or same-sex friendships won't do anything but rob us if they become a breeding ground for sexual sin. It's vital as believers that we know ourselves and one another well enough to know what true love looks like in a friendship—whether with a man or with a woman. In many cases, we will need to work with different boundaries, depending on whether we're relating to an opposite or same-sex friend.

> We should be fostering the kind of sibling love that we're commanded to in Scripture: love that seeks to serve and value others and to help them live in love and holiness.

But in every case, we should be fostering the kind of sibling love that we're commanded to in Scripture: love that seeks to serve and value others and to help them live in love and holiness. We need the Spirit's help with this, just as we need His help with every other aspect of the Christian life, so we must pray for guidance. But thanks to the Spirit, we belong together in the Lord, and we can live that out in friendship.

chapter nine

LOVING
NEIGHBORS

"We had a meeting at work today about having better conversations when we disagree. I thought of you and me! I think we do that well."

My neighbor Julia had just got off her bike after work.* We had become friends over the course of the previous year from picking each other's kids up from school and discovering in the process that we like each other. Julia is a pediatric anesthesiologist. Life-and-death decisions are her daily bread. This sometimes makes for stressful disagreements in the operating room. But like most

---

* Not the Julia I mentioned earlier in chapters 2 and 7!

humans, Julia also has to navigate important disagreements outside work, including in her friendship with me.

In some ways, Julia and I have much in common. Before training as a doctor, she studied classics at Harvard. Our academic background has a lot of overlap. We get each other's Shakespeare jokes. We value each other's feedback on our writing projects and help each other in a host of little ways. But while Julia and I have great respect for one another, we also have deep disagreements. Julia is Jewish and does not believe that Jesus is the Son of God. This is a radical divergence of belief. It impacts our views on eternity and morality, on truth and Torah, on mission and vocation, and (given her understanding of Judaism) on sexual ethics and abortion. These are not minor disagreements. Like the decisions Julia makes every day at work, they are matters of life and death.

In this chapter, we'll explore what friendship looks like between Christians and non-Christians—whether they identify as Jewish, Muslim, Hindu, Buddhist, atheist, or agnostic. We'll look at the importance of extending hospitality to those with whom we disagree, not only in the usual ways we understand that term, but also in the sense of listening attentively to what a friend believes and why. Sometimes, we'll need to recognize that friends with whom we deeply disagree

> If Christians grasp onto the Bible as their guide, how we relate to those who do not share our faith does not look like hostility, avoidance, disrespect, or even tolerance. It looks like love.

may be just as well-thought-out and driven by desire for good as we are.

This does not mean all views are equally true. If Julia is right on certain questions, I am wrong, and vice versa. But it does mean not demonizing those with whom we disagree, as if they couldn't be both highly intelligent and deeply compassionate while also profoundly mistaken. In fact, if Christians grasp onto the Bible as their guide, how we relate to those who do not share our faith does not look like hostility, avoidance, disrespect, or even tolerance. It looks like love.

LOVE YOUR NEIGHBOR

When asked, "Which commandment is the most important of all?" Jesus replied, "The most important is, 'Hear, O Israel: The Lord our God, the Lord is one. And you shall love the Lord your God with all your heart and with all your soul and with all your mind and with all your strength.' The second is this: 'You shall love your neighbor as yourself'" (Mark 12:29–31). This summary of the Old Testament law was likely not original to Jesus. In Luke, a Jewish lawyer gives a similar summary of the law (Luke 10:27). What is utterly radical is how Jesus then answers this lawyer's follow-up question: "Who is my neighbor?" Jesus responds with a story of self-sacrificing love across racial, ethnic, and religious difference. In the story, a Jewish man is robbed and beaten and left to bleed out by the roadside. Two Jewish religious leaders pass by and don't help. Then, a Samaritan shows up and cares for the victim. The Jews of Jesus' day despised the Samaritans, and vice versa. This story, known as the parable of the good Samaritan, defines the neighbor we are called to love as the exact kind of person we were raised to hate.

In the Sermon on the Mount, Jesus presses this expansive principle of love even further: "You have heard that it was said, 'You shall love your neighbor and hate your enemy.' But I say to you, Love your enemies and pray for those who persecute you, so that you may be sons of your Father who is in heaven" (Matt. 5:43–45). Christians should be known as Jesus' followers not only by our love for one another (John 13:35), but also by our love for those most hostile to us.

What does this love look like? "If your enemy is hungry," Paul writes, "feed him; if he is thirsty, give him something to drink" (Rom. 12:20). This hospitality includes things Jesus' first followers would have done: inviting those most hostile to their faith to share their food or hang out in their homes. It also extends to things belonging to our modern world. Loving our enemies today might look like coming to the defense of our ideological enemies when they're being unfairly attacked online or responding graciously when we're attacked.

Often, loving our enemies means patiently listening to those who think of Christians as foolish, immoral, or harmful, and asking gentle questions to find out more about what's shaped their perception, rather than immediately leaping to defend our tribe. Best-case scenario, it means building real friendships based on mutual love and respect, despite deep disagreement.

I dedicated my first book, *Confronting Christianity*, to my best friend in England. Natasha is not a Christian, but we've been very close since we met at age sixteen. We disagree on many fronts and there have been times over the years when that's been hard for both of us. But we also have a deep affection for each other and great mutual trust, which makes it worth continuing in friendship despite our fundamentally different beliefs. We know each other well enough and love each other thoroughly enough to trust each other with our hopes and dreams and fears and insecurities. Often, we have to take the other person's point of view and say (explicitly or otherwise), "If I believed what you believe, I'd feel that way as well." Natasha knows I long for her to turn and trust in Jesus. But I can't make her decision about Jesus for her. Part of my respect for her is recognizing that she gets to choose what she believes. But another element of my respect for Natasha and my other friends who do not trust in Jesus is believing that—as thinking people, not mere products of their backgrounds—they could also change their minds.

PERSUASION AND RESPECT

When Julia and I were first becoming friends, she kindly said she'd like to read one of my books, so I give her a copy of *Confronting Christianity*. As she received it, Julia warned me, "You know it's very unlikely I'll change my mind." I said, "I know." Since then, she's been generous enough to read drafts of books I'm working on and give me feedback. Like my other friends who are not Christians, Julia knows that out of care for her, I long for her to put her trust in Jesus.

If we truly believe that Jesus is the only hope that any human has for being saved from God's eternal judgment against sin, we cannot say we love our friends and not want them to come to Him.

What's more, we cannot just be silent—praying for our friends but never speaking up. In his second letter to the Corinthians, the apostle Paul writes, "Knowing the fear of the Lord, we persuade others. . . . For the love of Christ controls us" (2 Cor. 5:11, 14).

Persuasion doesn't mean coercion or manipulation. But it does mean Christians making the best possible case for faith in Jesus, both in what we say and in how we live. Rather than being disrespectful, trying to persuade someone to change their beliefs is a sign of respect, and we should do our best to make them feel respected, even as we challenge their beliefs. Writing to Christians facing fierce opposition to their faith, Peter urges, "In your hearts honor Christ the Lord as holy, always being prepared to make a defense to anyone who asks you for a reason for the hope that is in you; yet do it with gentleness and respect" (1 Peter 3:15). Of course, some people who aren't followers of Jesus will find our beliefs so utterly offensive that they won't want anything to do with us. But we can always offer love and hospitality to those who are not Christians as far as they are open to receiving it.

So, are there any limits on the ways that Christians should pursue relationships with nonbelievers? Yes.

TO EAT, OR NOT TO EAT

As the apostle to the Gentiles, Paul repeatedly addressed the question of how Christians should relate to those who worshiped pagan gods. Two potential responses would have been straightforward. Paul could have prescribed separation: have nothing to do with pagan neighbors, family members, work associates, or former friends. Alternatively, Paul could have recommended syncretism: Jesus is the Son of God, but it's okay to worship other gods as well to keep the peace. But Paul's answer is neither separation nor syncretism. It's shining. "Do all things without grumbling or disputing," Paul writes, "that you may be blameless and innocent, children of God without blemish in the midst of a crooked and twisted generation, among whom you shine as lights in the world, holding fast to the word of life" (Phil. 2:14–16).

Paul's "No" to syncretism is crystal clear. "You cannot drink the cup of the Lord and the cup of demons," Paul explains to the Corinthians. "You cannot partake of the table of the Lord and the table of demons" (1 Cor. 10:21). Joining non-Christians in worship—which often involved eating and drinking—was antithetical to faith in Christ. Paul pens a similarly passionate warning against syncretism in 2 Corinthians:

> Do not be unequally yoked with unbelievers. For what partnership has righteousness with lawlessness? Or what fellowship has light with darkness? What accord has Christ with Belial? Or what portion does a believer share with an unbeliever? What agreement has the temple of God with idols? For we are the temple of the living God. (2 Cor. 6:14–16a)

Belial is another name for Satan. Just as believers in the Old Testament were called to separate themselves from the pagan nations that surrounded them, so Christians were to separate themselves from the pagan worship that surrounded them. This passage is often used to counsel Christians against dating or marrying non-Christians. While this may well be one valid application of this passage today, it's unlikely that marriage is what Paul had primarily in mind. Rather, he is urging to Corinthians not to fool themselves that they are on the same side as their pagan neighbors or that they can continue to participate in pagan worship, now that they've been united to Christ. So, does this mean that Paul was teaching total separation between Christians and their pagan neighbors? No.

"If one of the unbelievers invites you to dinner and you are disposed to go," Paul writes, "eat whatever is set before you without raising any question on the ground of conscience" (1 Cor. 10:27). Eating with an unbeliever would have been a big deal for Paul, who was raised with the practice of not eating with non-Jews. Paul clarifies that it is not wrong for a Christian to dine with a non-Christian, even if the food has been sacrificed to idols. He goes on to explain that if the host explicitly declares, "This has been offered in sacrifice," Christians shouldn't eat, because it could make their host think they were joining him or her in pagan worship (1 Cor. 10:28–30). But Paul is happy for Christians to eat with non-Christians friends, so long as they are not causing confusion.

Paul is also keen that the Corinthians don't cause believers who were once idol worshipers to stumble by eating food that has been sacrificed to an idol and hurting the conscience of their brother or sister (1 Cor. 8:7–13). These guidelines mean that the exact same action might be right or wrong for a believer depending on the people they are with. Followers of Jesus need to operate in love both to non-Christian friends and to our brothers and sisters, who may have vulnerabilities we do not have. Paul concludes, "So, whether you eat or drink, or whatever you do, do all to the glory of God. Give no offense to Jews or to Greeks or to the church of God, just as I try to please everyone in everything I do, not seeking my own advantage, but that of many, that they may be saved" (1 Cor. 10:31–33).

We're not called to blend in or to check out, but to shine.

Paul was committed to coming alongside non-Christians and accommodating their culture as far as he could:

> To the Jews I became as a Jew, in order to win Jews. To those under the law I became as one under the law (though not being myself under the law), that I might win those under the law. To those outside the law I became as one outside the law (not being outside the law of God but under the law of Christ) that I might win those outside the law. To the weak I became weak, that I might win the weak. I have become all things to all people, that by all means I might save some. (1 Cor. 9:20–23)

If you, like me, are a Christian, we should be completely clear that we will only worship the one true Creator God, revealed in Jesus Christ. At the same time, we should be willing to set aside our own cultural preferences to come alongside the nonbelievers in our neighborhoods, schools, workplaces, and families. We're not called to blend in or to check out, but to shine.

So, what does this look like in the area where both the pressure to blend in and the impulse to check out can be the strongest?

DO ASSOCIATE WITH
SEXUALLY IMMORAL PEOPLE

In many people's minds today, the most offensive thing about Christianity is no longer Jesus' exclusive claim to be our only hope for right relationship with God (John 14:6). Rather, it's the New Testament's uncompromising claim that sex belongs only in life-long marriage between a man and a woman.

If this teaching is countercultural today, it was also profoundly countercultural in the first century. In the Greco-Roman empire, men were not expected to be faithful to their wives. They were free to sleep with prostitutes of either sex, to use enslaved people sexually, and to have sex with adolescent boys and adult men, so long as they took the active role. Christian sexual ethics came as a massive shock to this system. Christian men were required to live either as faithful husbands to one wife or in celibate singleness (like Jesus Himself). This limitation of sex to the lifetime commitment of male-female marriage was a non-negotiable distinctive of God's people. It was not an agree-to-disagree issue. So, how are Christians to relate to people who are not living by Christian sexual ethics? Paul answers this question in his first preserved letter to the Corinthians.

Paul references a previous letter in which he told the Corinthians not to associate with sexually immoral people, and clarifies what he did and did not mean:

> I wrote to you in my letter not to associate with sexually
> immoral people—not at all meaning the sexually immoral
> of this world, or the greedy and swindlers, or idolaters, since

then you would need to go out of the world. But now I am writing to you not to associate with anyone who bears the name of brother if he is guilty of sexual immorality or greed, or is an idolater, reviler, drunkard, or swindler—not even to eat with such a one. (1 Cor. 5:9–11)

Many Christians today think they shouldn't associate with non-Christians who aren't living according to Christian sexual ethics—especially if they're in gay relationships. But Paul is clear that this is not what he means. Instead, he's calling Christians not to associate with other Christians who are engaging in ongoing, unrepentant sexual sin.

By Jesus' standards, all of us are sexual sinners (Matt. 5:27–28). But Paul highlights the night-and-day difference repentance makes. In the very next chapter of 1 Corinthians, Paul once again lists various kinds of sexual and nonsexual sin as barriers to inheriting the kingdom of God:

Or do you not know that the unrighteous will not inherit the kingdom of God? Do not be deceived: neither the sexually immoral, nor idolaters, nor adulterers, nor men who practice homosexuality, nor thieves, nor the greedy, nor drunkards, nor revilers, nor swindlers will inherit the kingdom of God. And such were some of you. But you were washed, you were sanctified, you were justified in the name of the Lord Jesus Christ and by the Spirit of our God. (1 Cor. 6:9–11)

For me, as a Christian who has always experienced same-sex attraction, this passage has formed one section of the guardrail composed of multiple New Testament texts that explicitly categorize same-sex sexual relationships as sinful (see Rom. 1:24–32; 1 Tim. 1:8–11; Jude 7). But it has also acted like a banister for me to cling to for encouragement. Like my friend Rachel, some of the very first Christians came to Christ with a history of same-sex sexual relationships. Like her and every other sinner who repents and puts their trust in Jesus, they were washed, sanctified, and justified in His name.

Befriending a non-Christian who is engaged in sexual sin does not affirm them in their sin. They know we disagree with them in the most fundamental way. Likewise, our hope for our non-Christian friends is not that they would start to live by Christian sexual ethics without knowing Christ. It's that they would put all their trust in Jesus as the one who paid the price for all their sin—just as He paid the price for ours. If someone puts their trust in Jesus, He becomes the Lord of all their life. But we should not expect someone to live by Christian ethics before they've been united to Christ. And if we understand the gospel for ourselves, we should approach our nonbelieving friends not with a smug self-righteousness, but with profound humility.

REMEMBER, GOD HATES PRIDE

One of the most disorienting things for many Christians in the West today is finding that they're on the moral low ground in the eyes of their non-Christian friends and neighbors. In previous generations, Christians tended to be recognized as on the moral high ground. Maybe they were seen as unattractively judgmental.

But it was typical for those who didn't go to church to think of those who did as morally superior.

Today, that ground has shifted. Christians are more likely to be seen as morally inferior. Especially when it comes to sexual ethics, gender identity, and abortion, those who hold to scriptural beliefs about male-female marriage, the givenness of biological sex, and the right to life of unborn babies are seen by many as morally repugnant: equivalent to racist segregationists or hateful misogynists.

What's more, the growing recognition of the ways in which churches have historically been guilty of a range of sinful practices—from propagating racial oppression, to acting hatefully toward non-Christians who identify as gay or lesbian, to covering up sexual abuse—has led to an increasing sense that Christians are the antiheroes in our culture. When we stand for Christian sexual ethics today, we're seen as taking an absurd, unloving, and ultimately futile stand on the wrong side of history.

Some Christians have reacted to this shift by trying to fit in. The arguments for affirming same-sex marriage and self-determined gender identity can feel so compelling when the alternative is being accused of hateful bigotry—and when you're aware of the times when Christians *have* acted in hateful ways. Other Christians have reacted in the opposite direction: refusing to acknowledge any history of sin in the church and doubling down on genuinely hateful attitudes that contradict the love of neighbor Jesus calls us to pursue. They want to scramble back onto the moral high ground by blocking their ears to legitimate critique and shouting down the opposition. But Jesus calls us to another way.

In one of His most powerful parables, Jesus contrasts a man

who would have been seen as impressively religious with a man who would have been spurned as a shameful sinner. Jesus told this parable to "some who trusted in themselves that they were righteous, and treated others with contempt" (Luke 18:9). The story went like this:

> "Two men went up into the temple to pray, one a Pharisee and the other a tax collector. The Pharisee, standing by himself, prayed thus: 'God, I thank you that I am not like other men, extortioners, unjust, adulterers, or even like this tax collector. I fast twice a week; I give tithes of all that I get.' But the tax collector, standing far off, would not even lift up his eyes to heaven, but beat his breast, saying, 'God, be merciful to me, a sinner!' I tell you, this man went down to his house justified, rather than the other. For everyone who exalts himself will be humbled, but the one who humbles himself will be exalted." (Luke 18:10–14)

Jesus calls His followers not to self-righteousness but to humble recognition of our sin. We're called to cling not to the moral high ground but to Jesus. We're called to walk in humbleness before Him and before our nonbelieving friends. Our message is not, "We're so good, you really should become like us!" Our message is, "We're so bad we needed God's own Son to die for us. That offer's on the table for you too." Shortly after listing various kinds of sin that are against God's law—from things our culture would affirm, like same-sex sexual relationships, to things it would rightly condemn, like enslaving people (1 Tim. 1:10)—Paul declares, "Christ Jesus came into the world to save sinners, of whom I am the foremost" (1 Tim. 1:15). If we're following Jesus, then the basis for our friendships with non-Christians is not condescension, judgment, or self-righteousness, but humbleness and love.

For years, as I related to non-Christian friends, I kept quiet about the hard things in my life. I thought I'd point them best to Jesus by convincing them that I had everything together, that I wasn't struggling like they were. In particular, I didn't tell my non-believing friends about my lifelong history of same-sex attraction and the sense of loneliness and longing it was generating in my heart. I wanted them to think that Jesus was enough for me. He is enough. But I now think that I can point to Jesus best by being honest with my friends about my sins and struggles. I'm not here to say I have it all together. I am here to say that I need Jesus every single day. I need His help provided in His Word and through His people. I need my brothers and my sisters to embrace me and assure me of His love on days when I feel like I'm utterly unlovable, and I need them to correct me on days when I'm justifying my own sin.

> If we're following Jesus, then the basis for our friendships with non-Christians is not condescension, judgment, or self-righteousness, but humbleness and love.

One day, there will be no more sin and struggling. Jesus will wipe away every tear from my eyes (Rev. 21:4). But in the meantime, I hope to relate to my non-Christian friends with humility and love. I was honored that Julia thought of me as someone with whom she can disagree well. I'm honored by the people in my life who do not follow Jesus but are willing to be friends with me. My earnest prayer is that one day, I'll get to call these friends my sisters and my brothers. In the meantime, I will do my best to love them as my neighbor, and therefore—with Jesus' help—to love them as myself.

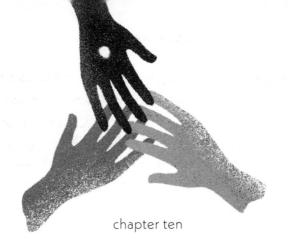

chapter ten

LIFE TOGETHER

In 1938, on the eve of World War II, German pastor-theologian Dietrich Bonhoeffer published a short book titled *Life Together*. By that point, much of the German church had sold out on Jesus to support Hitler. But Bonhoeffer was training pastors for the Confessing Church: a network of believers who refused to make their peace with Nazi evil. Living in makeshift housing with twenty-five fellow pastors who were risking their lives for their faith, Bonhoeffer described the blessings of Christian fellowship. But instead of painting an idyllic picture of a band of faithful brothers, Bonhoeffer made this startling claim:

> The serious Christian, set down for the first time in a Christian community, is likely to bring with him a very definite

idea of what Christian life together should be and to try to realize it. But God's grace speedily shatters such dreams.[1]

In this last chapter, we'll explore how we might live together in deep friendship in a world of shattered dreams. We'll examine what it looks like to lay down our lives for one another, what role forgiveness plays in Christian friendship, whether it is ever right to end a friendship, and how we can move forward when we've lost trust in each other or—perhaps yet more distressingly—in ourselves.

LAY DOWN YOUR LIFE

As we saw in chapter 1, when Jesus declared there was no greater act of love than someone laying down his life for his friends, He did so with full knowledge that His closest friends were just about to let Him down. His sacrifice for us was once for all. It set the perfect standard for extravagantly sacrificial love, and as high as the heavens are above the earth, so far above our little acts of service to our friends is Jesus' life-giving sacrifice. And yet He calls us to love one another in a way that mimics His great love for us (John 15:12–13). We can imagine what this love might look like in a life-and-death scenario: the kind of world in which Bonhoeffer lived and ultimately died for his faith. But most of us will never find ourselves confronted with the choice of whether we will literally die for our friends. Instead, we need to work out sacrificial friendship love in day-to-day decisions. One area where this should show is in consistent generosity.

When my friend Gloria was in business school, her negotiation professor set a surprising homework exercise: in the coming week, his students had to make three totally unreasonable requests. The purpose was to get them used to being turned down. So, Gloria texted a friend from church: "Can you give me $5,000?" Instead of saying no, her friend replied, "How soon do you need it? It will take me some time to get that much money together." Gloria tried again, asking another friend if she and her family could stay in her friend's apartment for a month. The friend agreed and asked for their dates. Time and again, Gloria failed to get rejections. You see, the people she was asking had known Gloria for years, and they knew she would give them anything if they needed it.

> Friendship is more precious than success. Friendship is more precious than popularity or opportunity.

Laying our lives down for our friends means sharing what we have: time, money, living space, vacation time, food, expertise, and family. It also means sharing in suffering: listening to a depressed friend's struggles, driving a friend with cancer to their chemotherapy appointment, sitting in silence with our arms around a grieving friend, skipping a social event we were excited to attend because our friend needs company. It even means sharing in our friend's exclusion. A friend of mine was once dropped by an organization she was meant to write for because of baseless slander about her theological beliefs. I was meant to write for the same organization, but I told them that if they didn't want my friend to write for them, they must also not want me, as she and I are in the same place theologically. Friendship is more precious than success.

Friendship is more precious than popularity or opportunity. We must be ready to stand with our friends when they're under attack. But we must also be prepared to suffer at the hands of our friends when sin crops up.

FORGIVE YOUR BROTHER

Given Peter's failure on that night Jesus was betrayed, it is ironic that it was Peter who had once asked Jesus what the limit on forgiveness was. "Lord, how often will my brother sin against me, and I forgive him?" Peter asks, "As many as seven times?" (Matt. 18:21). If we're honest, seven times sound like a lot. In marriage or in parenting, we might expect to have a regular rhythm of repentance and forgiveness, but in friendship, we have different expectations. In many cases, we'll just back away when we are hurt. But in response to Peter's question, Jesus raises the forgiveness ceiling to a cathedral-like height: "I do not say to you seven times, but seventy-seven times" (v. 22). This is extreme, extravagant forgiveness, flowing from God's extravagant forgiveness of us. So, what should this forgiveness look like day-to-day?

In the British comedy series *Miranda*, a character named Tilly is constantly picking up her phone in the middle of a conversation. While she texts other friends, she says to those standing right in front of her: "Bear with!" This habit is infuriating, but Tilly's catchphrase is a good one for the Christian life. Paul urges the Colossians, "Put on then, as God's chosen ones, holy and beloved, compassionate hearts, kindness, humility, meekness, and patience, bearing with one another and, if one has a complaint against another, forgiving each other; as the Lord has forgiven you, so you also must forgive" (Col. 3:12–13). Likewise, Paul instructs the Ephesians "to walk in a manner worthy of the calling to which you have been called, with all humility and gentleness, with patience, bearing with one another in love, eager to maintain the unity of the Spirit in the bond of peace" (Eph. 4:1–3). Patiently bearing with one another is part of Christian friendship. We should not jump on every opportunity to point out when a friend has hurt our feelings or frustrated us. We must, as Tilly would demand, "Bear with."

To bear with one another, it can help to notice when our friends must bear with us. For instance, I'm extremely punctual, so when a friend is late, I quicky find myself resenting them. I used to start an inner monologue. *Don't they care about my time? I'd never treat them like this! Can't they see how rude it is to keep someone waiting?* But while I am punctual, I'm also quite untidy. So, when a friend is running late, I try to remind myself, "Late for them is like untidy for me. They find it really hard." I do my best to bear with them, knowing there must be a thousand ways in which they're bearing with me. But this doesn't mean there isn't any room for actual accountability in friendship, or that forgiveness only comes in over-the-counter doses that can cover lower-level irritations. Peter's question comes right off the back of Jesus' teaching about how we should approach a brother or a sister when we've been significantly sinned against.

TELL YOUR BROTHER

The first step in Jesus' process is a private conversation: "If your brother sins against you, go and tell him his fault, between you and him alone. If he listens to you, you have gained your brother" (Matt. 18:15). It's tempting to default to other routes and turn to other friends to milk some gossip from the sin: "You won't believe what so-and-so did to me last week!" But we are only adding our own sin to the sin of our friend if we resort to gossiping about them (Rom. 1:29; 2 Cor. 12:20; 1 Tim. 5:13).

This doesn't mean it's never appropriate to seek wise counsel before bringing up a friend's sin. Sometimes, we need outside help to figure out if we are being sinned against, or if we're sinning. For instance, we might have a friend whose jealousy of our other friendships is causing them to sin against us by demanding that we put them first in any social situation. They might think we're the one at fault because they're feeling hurt when we make plans with other friends. But one person's hurt feelings doesn't always mean the other person has sinned. Sometimes, it takes talking things through with someone outside the situation to help us diagnose what's happening.

There have been many instances when I've felt hurt in friendship, and I've had to take some time to diagnose whether my hurt feelings have been caused by the sinful actions of my friend or by wrong expectations on my side—or just by natural differences. For instance, I'm an extrovert and many of my friends are introverts. There have been times when I've felt hurt by friends withdrawing from me in situations when, with roles reversed, I'd never have withdrawn from them. It's taken years for me to learn that they don't have the same thought processes as me. We tend to imagine other people think just like we do. But we are often wrong. A friend might truly love me and not make the same decisions I would make. So, we must be quick to extend the benefit of the doubt. But we must also be prepared to bring sin up when necessary.

Believe me, I hate conflict. I would almost always rather suffer someone treating me quite poorly than address their sin. I worry that if I bring up how a friend has hurt me, I will lose that friendship. So, I'm liable to suck it up and miss the opportunity for growth. You might be quite the opposite: too eager to bring up someone else's sin. It's vital that we all learn our base tendencies, so we can grow in our ability to surface conflict in a godly way. When Jesus instructs His disciples to address sin with each other face-to-face, He speaks as if the desired outcome is good for both parties (Matt. 18:15). Even as we bring up sin, we should do so with a desire for the other person's good. Where there is any doubt, we should begin with the assumption that we might have misunderstood their motives. Often, this will mean we take some time to sort through our emotions. When I'm hurt, I try to take some time to think through the extent to which my feelings are proportional before I bring them to my friend. "You hurt me, so now I'm going to hurt you back" might be my first instinct. But it's quite the opposite of how a Christian should behave.

> We must be quick to extend the benefit of the doubt. But we must also be prepared to bring sin up when necessary.

If there's a chance we don't have all the information, it's worth exploring that. For instance, we might start a conversation off like this: "I wanted to talk through what happened after church last week. I thought we'd agreed that you were going look after my kids, like I looked after your kids after church the previous week. But when I went out to the church playground, I saw my two-year-old had climbed way up onto the structure and was in danger, but you weren't around. I know you care about me and my kids, so I wanted to talk through this and understand what happened on your side." Of course, our friends are sinners just like us. But we should voice what we believe about their character and general good intentions toward us and give them every opportunity to help us see the context for their actions.

On the occasions when I have brought up conflict with a friend, I've mostly found that it's resulted in greater love and understanding on both sides. Sometimes, the friend with whom I've raised the issue has acknowledged fault and apologized, and we've both experienced the salve of forgiveness and reconciliation. Sometimes, they've explained their side and I've concluded that what I thought was sin toward me was more of a misunderstanding. Talking it through has helped us both understand each other's personalities and needs a little better. Sometimes, even after talking, we have disagreed, and I've had to let it go. I trust the Lord that often it is better to extend forgiveness even when a sin is not acknowledged than to hold on to a grudge. But there are times when sin is so substantial, ongoing, and unacknowledged that it warrants bringing others in.

SEEK HELP

Early one Sunday morning, I was standing outside our church building chatting with our pastor and another mutual friend when

Rachel started walking up the steps toward us. We all watched her approaching us. When she got to the top of the steps, she joked, "Is this an intervention?" It wasn't. But if she'd needed one, we would have been a decent lineup. When someone has significantly sinned against us and they don't repent when we bring it up with them, Jesus tells us that the next step is an intervention: "But if he does not listen, take one or two others along with you, that every charge may be established by the evidence of two or three witnesses" (Matt. 18:16). This step depends on one or two others in our community agreeing with us that our friend has sinned. We're not to raise an army to condemn our friend. Instead, we should seek counsel from a trusted friend or two and, if they think that we are right about the sin, we should approach our friend together with these other witnesses.

This step in the process is beneficial both for us and for our friend. It might be that we talk to one or two in our community who know us both, and they advise us that we've got it wrong. Perhaps our sense of being sinned against was more about our own agenda than the Lord's. We should seek people who have shown wisdom in relationships and who we know would tell us if we're out of line.

Sometimes, this process of bringing others into a situation requires a very detailed account of what has happened. Just as spousal relationships and parent-child relationships can be sites of emotional abuse, so too close friendships can be twisted in that way. It can be easy for well-meaning people who have not reviewed the situation carefully to move quickly to prescribing forgiveness and reconciliation without accountability, when in fact there's been an ongoing pattern of destructive sin that's grown up like a choking vine around the friendship. People who are experiencing emotional abuse will often struggle to articulate or even recognize that what is happening is not okay. If someone brings a situation to us, we will need to gently ask a lot of questions so that we can get a sense of what is really going on, and what the right next steps might be. We may discover that we're out of our depth and need to ask for expert help. The more we recognize that friendship can be a vehicle for extraordinary love, the more we'll also need to recognize that it can be a site of very serious sin.

If we believe that we are being sinned against in friendship and we bring it to one or two trusted advisers who agree with that analysis to the extent that it warrants an intervention, we should go with them to our friend and give him or her another chance to listen and repent. In cases of emotional abuse, the person who has been on the receiving end should be protected from the interaction and instead be represented by advisers. Jesus is clear that Christians cannot withhold forgiveness, even from their enemies. But forgiving someone does not always mean renewing an active relationship with them, and loving someone sometimes looks like holding them accountable. Sin doesn't only hurt the victim. It also hurts the perpetrator. Helping someone see their sin may prompt them to repentance, which is truly what is best for them, and sometimes an intervention from multiple people is required to help a brother or a sister see their sin.

Last weekend, our family went skiing. At one point, Bryan was skiing a hard run when he saw a woman slide right off the course and disappear over the edge. He skied down toward the place where he'd last seen her. She was standing about ten feet down, knee deep in freezing water. Two other skiers had come to help as well. "I'm fine!" the woman said. But it was clear that she was far from fine. She had no way to get out by herself, and if she stayed where she was, she could have ended up with hypothermia. So, they teamed up to reach down to her and help her get out.

It struck me that this moment was a picture of what we are called to do if we see a dear friend stuck in sin. It's not our job to stand there on the moral high ground shouting down to them about how wrong they were to go off course. It's also not our job to leave them where they are. We must team up to help. But ultimately, they will have to be willing to be helped. If the friend we've confronted refuses to repent, the next step Jesus specifies involves the broader church (Matt. 18:17).

Of course, the vast majority of conflicts between friends will not be on a level that requires this kind of intervention. This is a rare scenario. Usually, a private conversation is enough. When it is not, involving one or two wise friends will hopefully prompt repentance. But while forgiveness is required of us by Jesus and while faithfulness in friendship is one way in which we show the world His love, forgiveness does not always mean continuing in active friendship.

FRIENDSHIP FREEDOM

Some years ago, I lost a friendship that had been very precious to me. It had many of the features of Christian friendship I've described in this book: closeness built around shared mission with a fellow soldier. But after some time, my friend began to feel that

I was relating to her in unhealthy ways. She diagnosed a codependency in me that I was trying to fend off, but unsuccessfully. After praying and consulting with one or two people she trusted, she decided it would be best for both of us to end our friendship. The fact was, I had turned something that was good into an idol, and the Lord ripped that idol out of my hands.

My sister in the Lord did not owe me the deep friendship we'd once had. My own sin was the primary reason that our friendship got off track, and she exercised her freedom to step back. Deep friendship should not be relinquished lightly. But we should all commit to friendship knowing that while the other person is obliged to forgive us if we sin against them as they have been forgiven by the Lord, they're not obliged to carry on in close relationship with us. This is one of the respects in which close friendship is not like marriage. Freedom is baked into the relationship, and sometimes ending a friendship is the best thing for both parties—even if one party does not recognize that at the time. When we do lose friendships over sin on our part or someone else's, we have an opportunity to learn and bring that learning into future friendships.

In chapter 1, I quoted a passage from Bonhoeffer's *Life Together*: "Just as surely as God desires to lead us to a knowledge of genuine Christian fellowship," he wrote, "so surely must we be overwhelmed by a great disillusionment with others, with Christians in general, and, if we are fortunate, with ourselves."[2] When I lost that friendship that was so important to me, it was hard for me to trust again. But part of where I lost the trust was in myself. I needed to build back that trust with new foundations. I needed to more truly reckon with my tendency to hurtle into codependency.

I needed to distrust my feelings early in a friendship, sometimes putting on the breaks or leaning into other friendships even when the closeness felt so good. I needed to distrust myself and give myself the boundaries that I knew I'd need in the future, even if I didn't want them at the time. My dream of Christian friendship had been shattered. I had reached the point of disillusionment not first and foremost with my former friend but with myself. I needed to ask where I'd gone wrong and how the Lord had let what seemed so good come crashing down around my ears. When that close friendship started, I had thought the Lord was healing me, but really, He was breaking me to pieces in my sin.

> When we reach the point of disillusionment, Jesus will be there awaiting us with arms stretched wide.

As I've reflected on this season in my life, I've pondered on Hosea's loving invitation to God's people:

"Come, let us return to the LORD;
    for he has torn us, that he may heal us;
    he has struck us down, and he will bind us up.
After two days he will revive us;
    on the third day he will raise us up,
    that we may live before him." (Hos. 6:1–2)

Hosea was writing to God's people in the eighth century BC, when they had succumbed to idolatry and come under God's discipline. But his words call out to us today when we have gone astray in one way or another. If you, like me, have found yourself quite disillusioned with yourself in friendship, know that Jesus reaches out to you and offers you forgiveness and a fresh start. He is the one who knows you better than you know yourself and loves you in your sinfulness and hurt and shame. He is the friend of sinners, so He's not surprised when we trip up (Matt. 11:19). Sometimes, He's the faithful friend who wounds us (Prov. 27:6). But when we reach the point of disillusionment, Jesus will be there awaiting us with arms stretched wide. When we give and get forgiveness from our friends, we're tasting something of His love for us: the love of which there is no greater, the love that drove Him to lay down His life for His friends.

Bonhoeffer started *Life Together* with Psalm 133:1: "Behold, how good and how pleasant it is for brethren to dwell together in unity!" It is truly a beautiful thing when brothers and sisters live like this. But just as we will only come to resurrection on the other side of death, we'll only reach that final unity when we have first been broken on the jagged edges of our sin. I can't do Christian friendship without Jesus. Neither can you. Without Jesus' help, we'll fail at fighting the good fight. We'll cling to idols and form selfish inner rings. We'll hate the discipline of mutual accountability and love the snugness and superiority that comes from leaving others out. We'll play it safe because we cannot face the vulnerability of closeness, and so we'll miss the chance to find our very heart in friends who love the Lord with all of theirs.

Without Jesus' help, we can warp the bonds of friendship into sexual sin. We can turn friends into idols, and we can refuse forgiveness when our brothers or our sisters need it most. But with Jesus, slowly, tenderly, we'll be able to move forward in deep friendships that will draw us close to Him. And as we huddle together for warmth around the one who laid down His life for His friends, we'll see the fire of true friendship spring up even from the embers of our disillusionment. "Behold, how good and pleasant it is when brothers dwell in unity," wrote David. "For there the LORD has commanded the blessing, life forevermore" (Ps. 133:1, 3).

ACKNOWLEDGMENTS

In theory, I could have written my previous books without the support of my friends. In practice, I did not. But this book quite literally could not have been written without the people who have given me permission to share a snapshot of our friendship, including Rachel Gilson, Karolyn Park, Julie Ferrell, Lexi Miltenberger, Paige Brooks, Julia Rigney, Julia Rosenbloom, Laura Sanderson, Gloria Yu, Sam Allberry, and Yashar Adibnia. I'm very grateful for each one of them—and for so many other friends, whose love is such a blessing in my life.

I'm thankful to Trillia Newbell, Connor Sterchi, and the whole team at Moody Publishers for their hard work and patience with me in the process of bringing this book into the world. I'm also very grateful for the expert readers who took time to vet this book in draft form, including Sam Allberry, Rachel Gilson, Christopher Cowan,

Dani Treweek, and Ellen Dykas. Their feedback and correction have made this book better. All remaining errors are my own.

Finally, I'm deeply grateful for the people in my life who aren't my friends. My husband, Bryan; our children, Miranda, Eliza, and Luke; my parents, Nicholas and Christine, and my sister, Rose. This book seeks to theologically undergird and celebrate the ways in which the friend relationship is different from the love between a husband and a wife, or between parents and children. But the more that I reflect on friendship love the more I am convinced that all the different kinds of human love are precious pointers to the love God has for us—refracting its blinding light in different ways.

One day, all who have repented and believed in Jesus will get to feel that love of God in all its fullness, as we embrace the one who laid down His life for His friends. Until then, here's to every kind of human love and, in particular, to friendship.

NOTES

CHAPTER 1: NO GREATER LOVE

1. All names in this book are real names. Stories about named friends are told with their permission.
2. Melanie Stefan, "A CV of Failures," *Nature* 468, no. 467 (November 2010): https://www.nature.com/articles/nj7322-467a.
3. Johannes Haushofer, "CV of Failures," https://www.uni-goettingen.de/de/document/download/bed2706fd34e29822004dbe29cd00bb5.pdf/Johannes_Haushofer_CV_of_Failures[1].pdf.
4. C. S. Lewis, *The Four Loves*, in *C. S. Lewis Signature Classics: An Anthology* (New York: HarperOne, 2017), 780.
5. Aristotle, *Nicomachean Ethics* 8.1155a.
6. Aristotle, *Nicomachean Ethics*, book 8.
7. Lewis, *The Four Loves*, 780.
8. Dietrich Bonhoeffer, *Letters and Papers from Prison*, trans. Isabel Best et al. (Minneapolis: Fortress Press, 2015), 510–11.
9. Dietrich Bonhoeffer, *Life Together*, trans. John W. Doberstein (New York: HarperOne, 1954), 26–27.

10. See also, for example, Luke 14:12; Luke 15:6, 9; John 3:29.
11. Daniel K. Eng, "'I Call You Friends': Jesus as Patron in John 15," *Themelios* 46, no. 1 (April 2021): https://www.thegospelcoalition.org/themelios/article/i-call-you-friends-jesus-as-patron-in-john-15/.
12. The standard Greek lexicon of the New Testament defines *hetairos* as "a person who has something in common with others and enjoys association, but not necessarily at the level of a *philos*."

CHAPTER 2: NONTRADITIONAL FAMILY

1. Joseph H. Hellerman, *When the Church Was a Family: Recapturing Jesus' Vision for Authentic Christian Community* (Nashville: B&H Academic, 2009), 35.
2. Danielle Treweek, *The Meaning of Singleness* (Downers Grove, IL: InterVarsity Press, 2023), 232.
3. Rebecca McLaughlin, "Why I Don't Sit with My Husband in Church: Five Reasons to Separate from Your Spouse—and Sometimes Your Kids—on Sunday Mornings," *Christianity Today*, April 19, 2018, https://www.christianitytoday.com/ct/2018/april-web-only/why-i-dont-sit-with-my-husband-at-church.html.
4. Rebecca McLaughlin, "Make Sunday Mornings Uncomfortable: Three Rules of Engagement at Church," *Desiring God*, August 4, 2019, https://www.desiringgod.org/articles/make-sunday-mornings-uncomfortable.
5. See, for example, 1 Corinthians 5:1–13; 2 Corinthians 2:6; Galatians 6:1; Ephesians 5:11; 1 Thessalonians 5:14; 2 Thessalonians 3:6–15; 1 Timothy 5:19–20; 2 Timothy 3:5; and Titus 3:9–11.

CHAPTER 3: MY VERY HEART

1. Marisa G. Franco, *Platonic: How the Science of Attachment Can Help You Make—and Keep—Friends* (New York: Putnam, 2022), 242.
2. John uses *agapaō* every time he is describing himself this way except in John 20:2, when he uses *phileō*.
3. In a chapter on slavery in my first book, *Confronting Christianity*, I explored what this letter does and doesn't tell us about Paul's view of slavery.

4. See Daniel A. Cox, "The State of American Friendship: Change, Challenges, and Loss: Findings from the May 2021 American Perspectives Survey," Survey Center on American Life, June 8, 2021, https://www.americansurveycenter.org/research/the-state-of-american-friendship-change-challenges-and-loss/.

5. Franco, *Platonic*, 15.

6. Franco, *Platonic*, 244.

CHAPTER 4: COMRADES IN ARMS

1. J. R. R. Tolkien, *The Two Towers* (New York: Ballentine Books, 2012), 257.

2. "During the course of the first century, the minimum term of service for legionaries rose from sixteen years plus four years as reservists to twenty years plus five years as reservists." *Dictionary of New Testament Background*, ed. Craig A Evans and Stanley E. Porter (Downers Grove, IL: InterVarsity Press, 2000), 994.

3. J. R. R. Tolkien to Clyde S. Kilby, December 18, 1965, in *The Letters of J. R. R. Tolkien*, ed. Humphrey Carpenter (Boston: Houghton Mifflin, 2000), 366.

4. Tolkien, *The Two Towers*, 363–64.

CHAPTER 5: THE INNER RING

1. C. S. Lewis, "The Inner Ring," Memorial Lecture at King's College, University of London, 1944, https://www.lewissociety.org/innerring/.

2. Curt Thompson, *The Soul of Shame: Retelling the Stories We Believe about Ourselves* (Downers Grove, IL: InterVarsity Press, 2015), 138.

3. Lewis, "The Inner Ring."

CHAPTER 7: YOUR UNEXPLORED SELF

1. Russell Moore, "Will a Happy Marriage Prevent an Affair?," Russell Moore (blog), September 14, 2017, https://www.russellmoore.com/2017/09/14/will-happy-marriage-prevent-affair/.

2. Esther Perel, "Why Happy People Cheat: A Good Marriage Is No Guarantee against Infidelity," *The Atlantic*, October 2017, https://www

.theatlantic.com/magazine/archive/2017/10/why-happy-people-cheat/ 537882/.

3. Sarah Lyall, "Esther Perel's Business Is Your Business," *New York Times*, March 26, 2023, https://www.nytimes.com/2023/03/26/business/ esther-perel-couples-therapy.html?smid=tw-nytimes&smtyp=cur.

4. See, for example, A. Bruk, S. G. Scholl, and H. Bless, "Beautiful Mess Effect: Self—Other Differences in Evaluation of Showing Vulnerability," *Journal of Personality and Social Psychology* 115, no. 2 (2018): 192–205, https://doi.org/10.1037/pspa0000120.

5. Julie Beck, "The Friendship Files," *The Atlantic*, https://www.theatlantic .com/projects/friendship-files/.

6. Marisa G. Franco, *Platonic: How the Science of Attachment Can Help You Make—and Keep—Friends* (New York: Putnam, 2022), 24.

7. Franco, *Platonic*, 26.

8. Franco, *Platonic*, 72–73.

CHAPTER 8: BROTHERS AND SISTERS

1. Billy Graham, *Just As I Am* (San Francisco: HarperOne, 1997), 128.

2. It is possible that John gives us a counter example, when he begins his second letter, "The elder to the elect lady and her children, whom I love in truth" (2 John 1). While John may have been addressing an individual woman and her children, it is more likely that this is a literary way of addressing a whole church.

3. Soumaya Keynes, "What's the Best Age Gap in a Relationship?," *The Economist*, June 26, 2017, https://www.economist.com/1843/2017/ 06/26/whats-the-best-age-gap-in-a-relationship.

4. Rachel Gilson, *Born Again This Way: Coming Out, Coming to Faith, and What Comes Next* (Charlotte, NC: The Good Book Company, 2020), 76.

CHAPTER 10: LIFE TOGETHER

1. Dietrich Bonhoeffer, *Life Together: The Classic Exploration of Christian Community*, trans. John W. Doberstein (New York: HarperOne, 1954), 26.

2. Bonhoeffer, *Life Together*, 26–27.